above: The Annunciation Window
below: The Oxford Movement Window

THE REAL PRESENCE

A HISTORY OF THE ANNUNCIATION CHURCH

Stephen Plaice

First published in Great Britain by The Church of the Annunciation.

© Stephen Plaice 2014

Cover design: Steve Xerri
Additional photography: Peter Xerri, Nina Emett
Typeset by: dit@ntlworld.com

Printed in England by: imprintdigital.com
Seychelles Farm, Upton Pyne EX5 5HY, UK

ISBN: 978-0-9929490-0-6

for the people of the Annunciation
past, present and future

Stephen Plaice is best known as a playwright and librettist, especially for his acclaimed play *Trunks*, set in the Brighton of the 1930s. He has lived and worked in Sussex all his adult life. For seven years he was Writer in Residence at Lewes Prison. He is the co-translator of the philosopher Ernst Bloch's *The Principle of Hope* and *Heritage of Our Times*. Stephen lives in Brighton with his wife and three children, all members of the Annunciation family.

The Church of the Annunciation
89 Washington St, Brighton, East Sussex BN2 9SR

CONTENTS

Old men and old women shall sit again in the streets of Jerusalem, each with a staff in hand because of their great age. And the city shall be full of boys and girls playing in its streets. Thus says the Lord of hosts: even though it seems impossible for the remnant of this people in these days, should it also seem impossible to me?

Zechariah 8:4-6

PREFACE

IT IS APPROPRIATE that, in its 150th anniversary year, a history of the Church of the Annunciation should be written to celebrate its existence and work in the Hanover District of Brighton. The Annunciation has a remarkable story which almost perfectly follows the trajectory of the Oxford Movement, the Catholic Revival within the Church of England. But it also charts the rise of the community in which it was planted in 1864.

Over the last fifty years there has been a marked change in the demography of the area in which the Church of the Annunciation was first established as a mission to the poor. This history is undertaken partly to demonstrate why this small, now apparently insignificant church has a unique value, within Brighton and in the history of the wider Church of England, and why it should be kept open for future generations.

In 1914, Mother Kate, one of the Sisters of Mary who opened the retirement home for London Men in Brighton that was served by the Annunciation, described the church's special atmosphere:

> *There is a peculiar something about The Annunciation which seems to grip tight hold those associated with it, both Priest and people. They love it with an intense love; they are essentially part of it; they are as it were indissolubly linked and bound up with it.*

Many others have spoken and written about the first time they walked through the door and the immediate sense of knowing it was going to be their church. I am one of those, and it is the 'peculiar something' to which I hope to give some expression here.

For every church there is an anecdotal history to be told, revealing the personalities, the familial and singular joys and tragedies of its parishioners. Such a history was provided by the Annunciation's eighth vicar, Father Bullivant, in his centenary booklet in 1964. Readers are invited to return to that, and indeed to the Jubilee Book of 1914 compiled by the fourth vicar, Father Carey. Both sources were drawn on for this history, but I have focused on the larger picture, on the religious and social currents that have flowed through the church and the community over 150 years, and on the priests, the key personalities that have directed them.

In writing the history of any church, there is the danger that its day-to-day routine of prayer, office, worship, (even the unacknowledged sacrament of cleaning), will be forgotten, along with its regular festivals, meetings and societies. I apologise in advance that I cannot reflect sufficiently the vast prayer-engine that the Annunciation has been over time. Nor can I reference enough the routine endeavours the priests and laity have undertaken over fifteen decades, both in the church and in the community, assisted for much of that time by the Sisters of Bethany and of the Holy Name. Henry de Montherlant once wrote: 'happiness writes in white ink on a white page'. I would say the same about habitual religious observance.

I am very grateful to Father Michael Wells, the current priest in charge at the Annunciation, for inviting me to research material for a historical exhibition to mark the anniversary of the church. So compelling was its story, I found I had to write a complete history. The book has benefited enormously from Michael's sanguine oversight and helpful advice in the early drafts.

For help in my research, I would like to thank many long-standing parishioners of the Annunciation, especially Jan Stevens for tracking down the men of the Annunciation who served in The First World War, Bill Verrier for his recollections of the choir over six decades. Thanks also to Andrew Morgan, Brian Stevens, Rosemary Faulkner Mitchener, and Janet and Barry Hewlett-Davies for sharing their memories of Father Bullivant with me. My thanks to Joe Michel for his help in identifying and attributing many of the artworks in the church. Alexia Lazou, from Brighton & Hove Museums, generously offered me her expertise on Aubrey Beardsley.

I am also most grateful to the churchwardens John Brownfield and Sue Richardson who put the documentary records of the church at my disposal. Alas, these are not complete, and my research has been somewhat hampered by the fact that many of the documents, particularly those created around the 'historical flashpoints' of the church, the kidnapping of the statuary in 1903, and the departure of Father Hinde to Rome in 1910, for example, are missing. To whichever murky quarter and for whatever purpose they have been expropriated, the church would welcome their return.

I am indebted to John Bridger and Vicky Sharman for their typesetting skills, patience and hospitality. I would also like to thank Steve Xerri for the design of this book, and of the exhibition it accompanies, but most of all for our years of friendship. Lastly, I am grateful to my wife, Marcia Bellamy, for her musical and substantial contribution to the spirit of the Annunciation.

Stephen Plaice
Brighton 2014

INTRODUCTION

IN ORDER TO understand the history of the Annunciation and the Oxford Movement from which it sprang, it is important to grasp divergent strands of belief in the Church of England in the nineteenth century. Since the English Reformation at the time of Henry VIII, the Church of England had been a separate communion, with its own monarch at its head, as 'supreme governor'. It saw itself as part of a universal church, 'one holy Catholic and apostolic church', affirming the gospels and the faith of the early church, but not subject to Roman governance or Roman canon law. Its intention was to be 'united not absorbed'. The Roman Catholic Church, conversely, regarded the Anglican Church as part of its own communion that had broken away from it, that should be returned; and it held the Anglican Eucharist invalid. As it still does today, it viewed the Pope as supreme pontiff with power over the whole global Christian church.

In 1829 Parliament passed the Roman Catholic Relief Act, which effectively removed all substantial restrictions on Roman Catholics in the United Kingdom and Ireland.[1] In its wake, between 1833 and 1841, a group of university churchmen, most notably, John Henry Newman, Edward Pusey and John Keble, published a series of tracts, ninety in all, which re-explored the Catholic tenets and duties of Christianity. These writers and their supporters, first known as Tractarians, were seeking to return the Church of England to its pre-Reformation roots and to reconsider its relationship with the Roman Catholic Church. The Oxford Movement, as they later became known[2], broadly believed that the Anglican Church was one of three branches of the Catholic Church, the other two being Roman Catholicism and the Eastern Orthodox Church, which should be reunited in a single church. This 'branch theory' did not assume the surrendering of Anglican identity to Rome; but many members of the movement saw the Pope as the ultimate temporal authority.

The Oxford Movement laid great emphasis on the Blessed Sacrament, and on its power to reveal 'the Real Presence' of Christ, not only in the Eucharist itself, but also post consecration, if the Sacrament were 'reserved' for the purpose of adoration. The movement saw the mediation of the priesthood as paramount in this process. It promoted belief in the Apostolic Succession, the idea that the power to reveal these holy mysteries had been handed down in an unbroken lineage from the Apostles. Auricular confession to a priest was also regarded as sacramental.

These teachings ran directly counter to those of the Reformation, and to Protestant theology and practice in general. Thus the Oxford Movement, (and the more liturgically pro-active Cambridge Movement which sprang from it[3]), was vehemently opposed in the mid-nineteenth century by the burgeoning evangelical wing of the Church of England. The Church Association (disparagingly known by its opponents as the Church Ass, or as the Persecution Company Ltd) was formed in 1865 by the leading evangelical churches in direct response to the perceived threat of the Catholic Revival. This revival was also opposed by a broad alliance of non-conformist groups who went so far as to form Protestant Defence Leagues to counteract the increasingly elaborate ritualism that was developing among those promoting Anglican catholicity (though this ritualism was not originally advocated by the Oxford theologians). In the middle ground between these two polarizing factions, there was, as ever, a large constituency of centrist Anglicans, looking on, sometimes with bemusement, sometimes aghast, at the rising tide of sectarianism. It is the interplay between all these tendencies that informs much of the story that follows.

The Catholic Revival in Brighton was masterminded by Arthur Douglas Wagner, son of the Vicar of Brighton, Henry Michell Wagner. In 1848 H.M. Wagner had financed the building of St Paul's Church in West Street, Brighton. Two years later he installed his son Arthur as its first perpetual curate. But his son's religion was to prove very different from his own moderate churchmanship, which deferred to 'the quality' and to the practices of the established church. During his student days at Cambridge, Arthur Wagner had come under the influence of Catholic Revivalist thinkers, especially J.M. Neale. Consistent with the theology of the Oxford Movement, and with the social engagement of Neale's Cambridge Camden Society, Arthur Wagner now saw his ministry in building churches and establishing Catholic communions in deprived areas, where, free from the pew rent charged by proprietary chapels, they might experience the Sacrament, and be exposed to the truth of the Incarnation.

Wagner also keenly promoted Catholic liturgy and ritual in his churches, especially the adoration of the Sacrament. This was the initial intention of the Annunciation mission.[4] But this ritualism was not just cultivated because he believed the faith would best be conveyed to the poor and uneducated through visual spectacle. It was intended to honour and revere the 'Real Presence' of Christ in the Eucharist. Christ was to be received in splendour. Wagner consequently engaged clergy who were comfortable with the 'six points of ritual observance' – the adoption of the eastward position when celebrating

Holy Communion, the wearing of Eucharistic vestments, the use of the mixed chalice (of blessed water and wine) and wafer bread, and the use of portable lights and incense.

The cultural conflict between ritualism and evangelism in the nineteenth and early twentieth centuries has often been misrepresented as the struggle between 'high' and 'low' church. A great deal of confusion surrounds the term 'High Church'. Its origins seem political, denoting Tory religion for the Whig faction. It was used to describe the type of Anglican religion practised by the 'quality', in opulent surroundings, probably paying pew rents, as opposed to the 'Broad Church' espoused by the Whigs, which set no great store by ceremonial, tending instead towards a moderate and undogmatic Protestantism. The term 'High Church' is now commonly used to criticise highly ritualistic liturgy, the 'smells and bells' approach to worship, particularly that of Anglo-Catholicism. This is misleading. The Annunciation, for example, has always maintained a highly ritualistic tradition; but its fourth vicar, Father William Carey, writing in the Jubilee Book he edited in 1914, definitely does not consider it to be High Church:

> *The Annunciation has ever stood for the Catholic Faith and Catholic practice. Please God it will continue to do so. It knows nothing of High Church or Moderate Church, or any other variety of churchmanship. It stands for the whole Faith – undiluted, undisfigured, undefiled. Better by far, an empty church than one filled with those whose adherence is gained by watering down or paltering with the Catholic religion.*

However 'High Church' is used, it is mostly a lazy and unhelpful term, that overlaps very different ideas of worship. It will be set aside here, as far as possible.

The argument over ritualism was no Victorian parlour game. The issue was regularly and hotly debated in the national press, and, as we shall see, the Annunciation, a tiny church, became a focal point of that debate on more than one occasion. In the early twentieth century, the controversy around the Annunciation culminated in what became known as 'the church crisis in Brighton', when the vicar and his curates finally went over to Rome. Throughout these years, there were also frequent public protests encouraged by local Protestant Defence Associations in Brighton, London, Liverpool and elsewhere, which often turned violent. More than once, this violence was visited on the person of Arthur Wagner himself. He was attacked in the street, and, according to his obituaries, though there is no documentary record of it, even shot at. Unlike his father, he was not a figure of compromise, remaining impervious to the criticism and unpopularity he aroused.

Throughout the second half of the nineteenth century a game of cat and mouse was played over Catholic liturgical practice between Arthur Wagner and successive Bishops of Chichester. Their suspicion was that Father Wagner himself would follow in the footsteps of his mentor J.H. Newman (later Cardinal Newman) and take the congregations of his churches and missions with him across to Rome. Richard Durnford, the Bishop of Chichester, wrote in reply to Edward Pusey in 1877:

> *Mr Wagner does not conceal that circumstances may compel him to make his submission to Rome... Roman doctrine and even modern Roman decrees do not either repel or alarm him. I cannot regard his future course but with the greatest uneasiness.*

A fair number of Arthur Wagner's curates, several of them attached to the Annunciation, did indeed make their submission to Rome. This might lend credibility to the argument that his churches were initially intended as clearing-houses for Anglican priests and their congregations, to prepare them for transition to Roman Catholicism. But Wagner himself never did cross the Tiber.[5] Instead he fostered an Anglo-Catholicism in Brighton that has endured for a hundred and fifty years already, and more than a century beyond his death.

The central question in any history of the Catholic Revival, even in the case of a small church like the Annunciation, must be: was the intention of revivalists like Arthur Wagner to offer a Catholic tradition within the Church of England, or to undermine it and to return its congregations to Rome? This question is important because it asks a second one: was there a core of Anglo-Catholic belief, distinct from Roman Catholicism, that had its own programme and integrity within the Church of England?

I hope to illuminate these questions by looking at the story of a single mission that developed directly out of the ideas of Tractarianism and the Oxford Movement. As we will see, vehement, often violent, public opposition to the Catholic Revival continued for the best part of a century, at least until WWII. This history of the Annunciation shows the church, its priests and people, and sometimes the larger community around it, contending with that opposition while wrestling with its own relationship with Rome and with the established Church of England over succeeding generations, right down to the present-day. As a historical examination of one small parish, I hope it may go some way to explaining that struggle in the church and in wider society.

1. THE MUSTARD SEED

IN THE MIDDLE of the nineteenth century the Hanover district of Brighton was part of a stretch of downland known as Hilly Laine[1] with only a few isolated dwellings and market gardens. The landscape changed rapidly with the coming of the railway and the building of the railway-works in Brighton in the 1840s. The church-builder and evangelist Arthur Wagner (1824-1902) responded to this demographic change by commissioning the building of inexpensive housing to accommodate the influx of railway-workers.[2] He also erected a simple mission church to serve the new population of the hill. This mission was later to become, to give its full dedication, the Church of the Annunciation of Our Lord to the Blessed Virgin Mary. The architect was a local builder, William Dancy, who raised the original structure at a cost of five thousand pounds.

In the centenary booklet he compiled in 1964, Father Bullivant, the eighth vicar of the Annunciation, describes the opening day of the church:

> *The first entry in the register of the church is a Mass at 8 a.m. on August 15th 1864 (the Feast of the Assumption of our Lady). It was attended by 54 people and other services took place later in the day. The total collection was £221, 9s,11d. (This amount at the time would have bought four of the new houses then being built in the district).*

There were four services at the mission on a Sunday, and the numbers grew steadily to begin with. J.M. Neale preached to a full house at the Annunciation on Lady Day 1865. At the end of the first year, the congregation for the Sunday Eucharist was 184, with a choir of 38. But many of these were children, and only about forty of the congregation took communion. From the beginning, a Eucharistic fast was imposed on communicants, which meant abstinence from food from midnight on the Saturday.

Miss Charlotte St John, a Sunday School teacher, whose memorial plaque is situated above the present crèche, recalls the early days of the church. She was only nine years old at the time of the events she is describing:

> It was on a Sunday evening in September, 1864, that we first heard the little bell. 'That must be Mr Wagner's new church,' we said, and started out to find it. The sound led us up Islingword Road, – Washington Street was only half built and impassable, Coleman Street little more than a white chalk path, – but we at last managed to find the entrance. I remember well going into the brightness of the little church from the darkness and dreariness outside: even in those far-off days there seemed to be something of the feeling of home and rest which we who love the Annunciation know so well now. It was the simplest little church imaginable – rough white-washed walls, the roof bare rafters, the stalls unpainted deal. The altar alone was dignified.

From the outset, the involvement of children increased rapidly. A lack of alternative diversion in their impoverished lives might explain their interest. The church would have provided an enticing alternative for a child to a damp, overcrowded and often disease-threatened house on a wet Sunday. Mother Kate describes one of the peculiar effects of the building:

> The colouring and structure of the Church lends itself to the picturesque. If you notice on a bright summer morning, you may see a long solid ray of light streaming from the clerestory windows in the sanctuary in one straight line to the ground, touching up the priests' vestments with a glory of colour, and looking like a pathway on which you would not be surprised to see Angels floating up and down; and this bar of light is more accentuated as all around you is more or less shrouded in mysterious grey and purple shadows. It looks like a golden ray of prayer ascending from the darkness, and passing out of our sight.

The early Annunciation made no secret of its ritualism. One of the first photographs of the church shows one of the rafters inscribed with the verse from Revelation (4:5)

There were seven lamps of fire burning before the throne which are the seven spirits of God

Even when it was still a bare mission, the overall intention of the space, with its sudden shafts of light, was to encourage spectacle. For the poor of what was to become Hanover, the Annunciation was their theatre, a kind of proto-cinema.

With the planting of the mission also came the building of schools. At first, provision was made for a School for Girls and Infants below the church (open to the air on three sides), and in 1865 plans were lodged for the building of a Boys School further up the hill in Southover Street. It is now the Hanover Community Centre. The teaching in the schools was resolutely Catholic, and there were regular visits by the children to the church, as part of the curriculum.[3]

At one of the services on the opening day of his new mission, Arthur Wagner preached on The Parable of the Grain of Mustard Seed:

today we are planting a seed amidst obloquy and opposition - may it grow to become a tree where souls may find rest.

Though he was a great mission-builder, Arthur Wagner, by all accounts, was not a great preacher. He was short-sighted and had to hold his notes close to his eyes to deliver his sermons. His themes were often too lofty for the uneducated congregations he preached to. But on this occasion Arthur Wagner's sermon proved eloquent and foresightful. It envisaged the flourishing church the little mission on the hill would become, but also the public confrontation it was about to inspire.

2. PUSSYBITES

The Annunciation was initially nothing more than an outpost of St Paul's, Brighton. Wagner put it in the hands of two of his curates – the Reverends Christopher Thompson and Charles Anderson. From the beginning, their teaching affirmed the real and objective presence of Christ in the Eucharist and devotion to the Virgin Mary. At this time, Sussex, was staunchly Protestant, with strong evangelical and nonconformist factions. Arthur Wagner was already attracting national protest for the liturgical practice he had introduced at St Paul's, and many people in the local area did not take kindly to having its annexe planted on their doorstep. The Brighton Protestant Defence Association (a forerunner of the Church Association) had specifically been established as early as 1856 to combat ritualism and Wagner's ministry in particular. Many local Anglicans believed that the kind of Catholic Revivalism Arthur Wagner was promoting was a kind of Trojan Horse inside the Church Of England.

Gradually Wagner introduced more and more elements of the Catholic Revival. He encouraged auricular confession, regarding it one of the sacraments, that of penance. This in itself was a controversial issue in the eyes of the church's Protestant and non-conformist opponents, who disagreed with the idea of priestly mediation and the 'seal of confession', the confidentiality between priest and penitent that was beyond the reach of the law.[1]

To begin with the priests at the Annunciation wore simple surplices and black stoles, but eventually Father Thompson collected enough money to invest in a white chasuble. The Annunciation then inherited scarlet vestments from St James' Chapel in Kemptown. These garments already had a contentious history. Along with other 'idolatrous' Catholic practices introduced by the Reverend James Purchas at St James', the wearing of such vestments had recently been the subject of legal controversy and even rioting. Arthur Wagner had publicly fought in Purchas' corner, publishing a letter in *The Times* criticizing the secular judiciary for interfering in church affairs. It was therefore no surprise that the offending garments and many of the ritualistic practices and artefacts found a new home at the Annunciation after Purchas' death in 1872. Their introduction inevitably further stoked the opposition of the mission's sectarian opponents.

Given the large number of children, a Sunday School was started in 1867. Not all those who attended at first did so for the best of motives. Older boys were sometimes sent in by the locals to disrupt the teaching with their mockery. Charlotte St John describes further obstacles that were put in the early congregation's way:

> *The neighbourhood was very rough, and there being at that time a great outcry about Puseyism, there was much opposition. The sight of anyone on their way to Church was the signal for shouts of "Pussy" or "Pussybite", and on Good Friday, when the custom of skipping in Brighton was even worse than it is now, they would stretch ropes across the road in the hope of making churchgoers skip.*

The strength of this local opposition may have contributed to the fact that the mission began to falter at the end of its first decade[2]. But there were other factors too. In the early days the Annunciation relied on the central energy of its priests. Father Anderson was destined for a greater career than a humble curacy in a mission church could provide. He left the Annunciation in 1871 to become senior curate of St Anne's, Soho, and was later to become vicar of St John's, Limehouse.[3] After eleven years service, Father Thompson left the mission in 1875, taking his musical expertise with him. He too went on to greater things, first at St Bartholomew's, Moor Lane, and subsequently as vicar of St James the Great in Pensax, Worcestershire.

But perhaps the biggest factor in the mission's decline was the erection by Arthur Wagner of a new and much grander temple, that of St Bartholomew's,

Brighton, which dominated the skyline north of the Steyne from 1874. Those in search of ritualistic religion were unlikely to eschew the splendour of 'the tallest nave in Europe' for the humble rafters of 'the barn' (the nickname given by its opponents to the Annunciation at the time). Consequently, the number of communicants at the mission dropped dramatically, as did the financial contributions from the congregation. Yet, curiously, perhaps because of the schooling that was now on offer, the number of children continued to grow, rising to over two hundred by 1875. Nevertheless, none of the curates who were sent up to the Annunciation from St Paul's could make any further headway with the mission. They found little local support and quickly moved on. The sung Sunday Mass was discontinued in 1875 except for feast days, and said mattins became the main service of the day. On Easter Sunday there was only one Mass which a mere 29 people attended. By Christmas that year the numbers were worse, only 18 were present at the single early morning Mass. Arthur Wagner's mission on the hill might easily have bowed to the continuing local sectarian opposition and disappeared altogether, were it not for the arrival of the man who is still regarded as the spiritual father of the Annunciation today – Father Chapman.

3. FATHER CHAPMAN

I N 1877, THE AREA we now know as Hanover was developing rapidly.
It was already unrecognisable from the ramshackle landscape of a decade
earlier when the mission had first been raised. But with urbanization
came poverty and disease. Charlotte St John described this period, when
she was still a young woman:

> *There was no parish then, Brighton being all one parish; but as the
> Annunciation was the only church north of St Peter's, the Clergy were liable
> to be called in all directions, especially for infectious diseases, which were then
> very prevalent. A lady who had a child ill with scarlet fever was in despair
> at being unable to get a Priest to visit her. 'Send to the Annunciation', she
> was told, 'you will not be refused there'; and so she found. I can remember
> being warned to walk in the middle of the road in Washington Street as
> small-pox was raging there.*

Arthur Wagner's task was now to find a priest who would be able to cope
with such conditions. He knew he was unlikely to find an unflinching crusader
into poverty from among his existing curates. Astutely, he chose to appoint
George Chapman, a young Liverpudlian fresh from a curacy in dockland
Liverpool, where he had already become highly experienced in the pastoral

care of families and individuals living in deprived and squalid circumstances.

Father Chapman's early letters betray a reluctance to leave his native city; he even suffered bouts of homesickness. Nevertheless, he threw himself wholeheartedly into his new ministry. Upon his arrival, there were only twenty adults in the congregation at the single celebration of Holy Communion; but there were still many children in the Sunday School, which gave him cause for hope. Charlotte St John recalls the occasion:

> *His first words to me on that first Sunday were altogether characteristic: 'If we begin a daily Celebration, can you promise to come every day?' Mr Wagner had told him it was hopeless to have a daily Mass, as no one would come; but Mr Chapman had answered, he must try, as he could not starve his own soul. So he began it, and it has never failed since.*

Chapman saw himself as an 'Evangelical Catholic', whose first task was to fill the pews. He set about this by holding 'mission' services, characterised by vigorous hymn-singing and short, robust preaching. He told his assistant priest Edwin Green on the latter's arrival at the church:

> *What I want is, what I may term, earnest Wesleyan preaching on Catholic lines; we must get at people's hearts before they can be led on*

The preaching nevertheless remained distinctly Catholic and strongly focused on the Incarnation. Alongside these popular services, pitched to suit his poor, largely uneducated congregation, Father Chapman quietly began to introduce ritualistic elements of the Roman Catholic Mass into the daily liturgy. R.S. writes about the curate's early years at the Annunciation:

> *So the three years of his curacy passed on; the souls under his charge were gradually trained in Catholic doctrine and practice. Before any change was made in the services he talked to them about it, giving plain reasons for the change, so that they learned to desire it.* [1]

Father Chapman began to impress on his flock the sacramental necessity of confession to a priest. These confessions were heard in the organ chapel. Father Chapman used to move among his congregation before Mass and select likely penitents. It gave him a unique control over their lives; and a level of public trust began to be placed in him that went far beyond his own flock. His tall, lean figure in its shabby rusty-black cassock was generally respected by all, regardless of their denomination. He was a thoughtful gift-giver, and yet expected nothing in return, living ascetically to the point where he ignored his own well-being, and ultimately his health. 'I will have nothing for myself', he is recorded as saying when his landlady urged him to accept a silver inkstand that was offered him to replace a decrepit one. Father Chapman's ministry to the people of Hanover bordered on, some would say even crossed over into, the saintly.

Yet, George Chapman was not without a temper. Since childhood, he had been prone to sudden outbursts of rage. His indignation was roused if any disrespect was shown to the Sacrament: 'Kindly and compassionate at other times, he would then seem stern almost severe', the author of his first memorial, 'One of his People' remembers. 'We must deny our bodies', he exhorted his flock in Lent, tapping his foot irritably against the wooden pulpit if anyone dozed off in his sermon. We may choose to view this irascibility as 'righteous anger', the same anger Christ displayed when removing the moneylenders from the temple, but it was genuine anger nonetheless. Neither was Chapman an admirer of what he called 'the carriage folk', the affluent townspeople whom he felt should confine their worship to the Chapel Royal and St Peter's.

In her biography of the priest, R.S.[2] has left us a description of Father Chapman moving among the ordinary working people of Hanover in the early morning:

> *Everyone was at home with him. He made his people love his church; the poor man was encouraged to go there on his way to work, to say his morning prayers, to use the church, indeed as his private chapel, because, he would say, 'in their crowded homes, what chance have they of a moment's quiet, when they can be alone with God?' And so at five o'clock, even on the chill, dark mornings of early winter, he would generally manage to be there dusting and tidying, and any who availed themselves of the ever-open doors of their little church – and some did – would be sure of a warm shake of the hand, and a hearty 'good-morning', and went on to their day's toil all the brighter and happier for the fervent 'God bless and keep you', from their pastor's lips and heart.*

Attendance at the church recovered remarkably quickly after Father Chapman's arrival. By Lady Day 1878, a year into his ministry, there were in excess of three hundred in the Sunday Mass, 71 of whom were communicants. He founded the Annunciation Church Society in that same year. The society required every member to pray daily, to come to Mass on the first Sunday of the month and to attend a monthly meeting. Practically, it became the first roll of communicants.[3] George Chapman's successful ministry did not go unnoticed by the Bishop of Chichester. Hanover was now a bustling working-class community that deserved separate status from the parent church of St Paul's. It was ready to become a parish.

4. EXPANSION

ARTHUR WAGNER'S project for the Hanover area took a step further forward, when, on Lady Day 1880, the Annunciation was granted full independent parish status[1]. After his customary spiritual deliberation, George Chapman agreed to be its first parish priest. It was a triumphant moment both for him and for Father Wagner. The Annunciation had now patently fulfilled the ambitions of the Oxford Movement in a parish context, reviving pre-Reformation, Catholic Christianity and creating a Eucharistic community from scratch. It is one of the most perfect historical examples of the practical phase of the movement, when the theological ideas developed by Newman, Keble and others in the 1830s and 1840s (together with the aesthetic vision for liturgical reform envisaged by J.M. Neale) were put into practice in poor areas by socially-engaged priests like Father Wagner.

Father Chapman's next move was to purchase two cottages adjoining the church. These were converted into the first Clergy House, making it easier for the clergy to be on hand at any time of day when help was required by a member of the congregation. In 1882, Chapman received the parochial help he had long desired, in the form of two nuns from the London-based Sisters of Bethany.[2] Their presence in the local streets, and the practical help they were able to offer struggling families further enhanced the pastoral reputation of the Annunciation, and seemed to assuage, temporarily at least, the sectarian tension surrounding it.

It was largely down to George Chapman's tireless and successful efforts in attracting communicants that Arthur Wagner now proposed to build a larger church on the site. When, at the beginning of the 1880s, Wagner offered to rebuild on a grander scale, Father Chapman told him that the parishioners were very fond of the little church as it was, and suggested instead the enlargement and improvement of the existing building. We have this account from the reliable Father Edwin Green. Given what we now know of Chapman's ascetic character, we may speculate on whether this was indeed the wish of the congregation, or merely Chapman's own interpretation of it. In any case, the wish prevailed.[3]

The architect of the renovation was Edmund Scott, a man with a greater pedigree than the local builder who had erected the original structure. Scott had raised Wagner's grandiose St Bartholomew's in 1874. From 1881 he added the north aisle and the Holy Name Chapel to the Annunciation and remodelled the existing south and east walls. Much of the stained glass we see today was installed at this time, many of the windows memorialising ordinary contemporary parishioners, among them one of the St John family.

In 1883, as an acknowledgment of the success of the Catholic Revival within the Church of England, the major feature of the extension, the stained glass west window, was dedicated to John Keble and Edward Pusey, leading lights of the Oxford Movement, both of whom had been personal friends and mentors of Arthur Wagner. This window, by an unattributed artist, has been somewhat overlooked in favour of the Burne-Jones Annunciation window above the High Altar. But in one sense it holds the key to the understanding of the church. The dedication running across the bottom of the triple lancet reads:

In thankful recognition of the many mercies to the Church of England between the years 1833 and 1883. In loving memory of his servants the Rev J Keble and the Rev E B Pusey whom may God abundantly reward.

The date 1833 is significant, being the year John Keble delivered his speech on 'National Apostasy' in Oxford, and generally acknowledged as the beginning of The Oxford Movement. So the window marks the fiftieth anniversary of the movement as well as the expansion of the mission. Keble and Pusey had only recently died. How fervently Arthur Wagner must have wished to add the name of the Roman Catholic convert John Henry Newman's to the glass to be honoured in their company. Wagner had recently been present at Newman's ordination as cardinal in the Holy City in 1879. But to have publicly honoured him in an Anglican church would perhaps have only given further ammunition to the Annunciation's sectarian opponents. And Newman, of course, was still very much alive.

For Father Wagner, George Chapman's successful incumbency must have been a vindication of his decision to plant the church in an area initially so hostile to Catholicism. With the expansion of the original building into the present church, its consecration and the creation of the parish, there was the sense that the 'mission' had truly been accomplished.

The enlarged church was finally dedicated on July 9th 1884 under the expansive title of The Church of the Annunciation of our Lord to the Blessed Virgin Mary. The consecration was performed by Bishop Tufnell, Assistant Bishop to the Diocesan Bishop Richard Durnford. Durnford himself came to preach at the evening service. It was only seven years since he had expressed his suspicions of Wagner's intentions to Edward Pusey. These suspicions had still not entirely been allayed. During his sermon, the bishop admired the church's 'beautiful pictures', by which he meant the Stations of the Cross. The remark was not without its subtext. The Catholic practice of visiting the Stations of the Cross was not condoned by the Diocese.[4] In the Bishop's observation we may detect the continuing tussle over ritualism that had been going on between Chichester and Wagner for the previous three decades. But, as we shall see, Durnford's ambivalence towards Wagner's project did not prevent him from defending its Marian tradition when necessary against desecration by its militant Protestant opponents.

According to his biographer, R.S., Chapman went out of his way to pursue souls in whom he saw the gleam of faith, particularly young men, whom he called his 'boys'. Among this flock was the pubescent artist, Aubrey Beardsley, the future art editor of *The Yellow Book*, the infamously 'decadent' literary periodical which was at the forefront of fin de siècle aestheticism in England. Twelve-year-old Aubrey and his thirteen-year-old sister Mabel (who later became an actress) lived with their seventy-year old aunt, Sarah Pitt at 21 Lower Rock Gardens. Their mother, Ellen Beardsley, wrote: 'Their chief interest (during the five months, August 1884 until January 1885) was in going to church, a very high church, "The Annunciation" in Washington Street.' Fred Carr, a master at Brighton Grammar School which Aubrey attended, suggests that there was a very close relationship between the First Vicar of the Annunciation and the young Beardsley. In 1920, the retired schoolmaster wrote:

I remember on one or two occasions taking him to Sunday Evensong to the Church of the Annunciation in Washington Street, Brighton, of which church Revd Father Chapman was vicar. Father Chapman was, I believe, Beardsley's guardian, a man of what were then considered most advanced views which then appealed strongly to Beardsley.

What seems to have left the most lasting impression on Beardsley was the vivid catholicity of the church. By all accounts, life for the young Beardsleys with Miss Pitt was devoid of colour and interest. After visiting them in their Brighton accommodation, Ellen's father, the Surgeon-General William Pitt complained to his daughter about her children sitting on their 'little high-backed chairs' with nothing to do. No wonder they were keen to attend the Annunciation. The Beardsley children appear to have attended the church of their own volition, climbing the steep hill to Hanover more than once on a Sunday to worship, and to escape the confines of Miss Pitt's domicile.

Sadly, George Chapman left no account of his encounter with these gifted children. They must have been a brother and sister among so many. Neither would the vicar have approved, we imagine, of Beardsley's later 'decadent' contributions to *The Yellow Book*, nor of the fact that the artist ultimately chose the Roman Church, rather than his own. But he never lived to see Aubrey's ground-breaking work published, nor to hear of his young protégé's conversion. Despite the scurrilously erotic (for the time, pornographic) nature of his drawings, Beardsley became a Roman Catholic in 1897, a year before his death. There is one work of the artist's, sometimes referred to as *The Annunciation,* but traditionally given the title *The Mysterious Rose Garden*, which seems to have a sense of the momentous meeting between Gabriel and the Virgin Mary. It appeared in volume IV of *The Yellow Book*. It shows an angelic figure whispering into a naked woman's ear. Could it be a subliminal memory of Beardsley's for the Burne-Jones window that he must have gazed on many times as a boy worshipping at his favourite church?

Unfortunately, Beardsley and his first priest were to suffer the same fate, both falling victim to tuberculosis (the artist at the age of only twenty-five). A lifetime working in cold squalid parishes and draughty churches had inevitably taken its toll on Father Chapman. In the late 1880s he was diagnosed with what was then known as consumption. Several holidays in Switzerland, Italy, Scotland and the Isle of Wight failed to improve his condition, as did a visit to Italy and Rome (where he caught a glimpse of Leo XIII on two occasions, and was shown the papal vestments by the Pope's chamberlain). Chapman was always anxious to return to the fray, insisting on continuing all aspects of his parochial work, if anything with renewed vigour. He died of a haemorrhage of the lung in 1891 in the midst of his busy ministry, having just heard confession. He was only forty-four years old. The Reverend Edwin Green witnessed the onset of the fatal attack:

> *To breathe his last within a few minutes after exercising the Priestly Office in the Confessional, and to know his call had come while kneeling before the Blessed Sacrament in the Oratory, was indeed to die in the harness he had put on at his ordination. As he came down from his Confessional that last Friday he was to have on earth, I was at the Vestry door, and I noticed that as he passed the porch entrance he stayed to unhook the heavy draft padded curtain which was generally left so in the day-time. Remembering what took place a few minutes afterwards I cannot help thinking that this lifting up his hands to release the weight (an action well-known to be dangerous to anyone with weak lungs) must have started the flow of blood from his lungs which removed the dear Father to the Church Expectant.*

Whether by accident or design, the subliminal analogies with Christ in the description of Chapman's death are unmistakable – the last Friday, the tearing down of the curtain and the blood. The iron nails that held up the curtain are still visible today above the entrance arch into the nave. Coincidentally, it is precisely in this location that, on Holy Saturday, at the beginning of the Easter Vigil, when the Easter Fire is lit, five nails, symbolic of those used to pinion Christ to the Cross, are driven into the Paschal Candle. (Here too, on the wall, is set Father Chapman's memorial). Nor was Edwin Green the only one to hold Father Chapman in Christ-like regard. The comparison with Christ is further reinforced in *Some Brief Recollections of the late Reverend George Chapman,* a memorial volume compiled by 'One of his People' and published not long after Chapman's death.[5]

> *Of the vicar it has frequently been remarked: 'How like the pictures of our Lord', 'What a Christ-like face'. Simple, unlettered folk have said the same, only expressing it after their own fashion. One poor woman, speaking of him to her District Visitor, said: 'I beg your pardon, ma'am, but don't you think he looked so much like the Saviour?'*

A traffic-stopping procession followed his body from the church to its final resting place in the Lewes Road cemetery, testimony to the general respect he had engendered that transcended sectarian division.[6]

By the time of Father Chapman's premature death, the Annunciation Church Society had admitted 290 men and 600 women, a huge proportion of the local population. When asked about the discrepancy in the number of women over men, the First Vicar had responded:

> was it not always so, even at the foot of the cross, where three women and only one man awaited the end, and is not a woman's soul as precious in God's sight as a man's?

Even today one can still sense the enormous effect that Father Chapman had on the Annunciation, but it is still easy to underestimate the transformational impact he had on the wider area of Hanover. A testament to how dramatically he turned the parish around is given by his biographer R.S., writing in 1893, only two years after his death.

> The rough people in the parish, in their ignorance and blindness, resorted to violence such as seems hardly credible now. The clergy and choir attempting to walk in procession through the parish, were mobbed, and an attempt made to burn them by setting their surplices on fire. Friendly people came to the rescue; the boys were taken into houses, and their surplices removed, and Mr Chapman was forcibly pushed into the church and the doors shut and held by strong men. It is difficult for anyone who was present at the vicar's funeral some fourteen years afterwards, and witnessed the reverent order of the dense crowd collected on that occasion, to believe this; but it was even so; the whole tone of the parish altered soon after Mr Chapman began to work there.

Had he been a Roman Catholic, Chapman would, I believe, have been a strong candidate for sanctification, though his miracles were social ones. The Reverend Rocksborough 'Rocky' Smith, the Annunciation boy who later became a bishop, describes him in the 1914 Jubilee Book as 'dear saintly Father Chapman, the Father, above all others of mortal frame, to all who were privileged to know him.'

5. THE REAL PRESENCE

ONE CANNOT REALLY understand the impending troubles at the Annunciation without considering two related issues of crucial importance in the nineteenth century that divided not only Catholics and Protestants, but also ritualistic and 'centrist' Anglicans: the Reservation of the Sacrament and 'the Real Presence'.

The Reservation of the Sacrament

The Reservation of the Sacrament concerned the further use of the Host after it had been blessed and distributed in the Eucharist. The ostensible purpose of this Reservation was to administer it to the sick and the dying, i.e. in extremis. But it also allowed the possibility of further veneration of the 'real presence' of Christ which had been effected through transubstantiation. The idea of Reservation was abhorrent to the militant Protestant defence leagues, who regarded it as idolatrous.

Reservation was largely prohibited in the Church of England after the Reformation[1]. In the Thirty-Nine Articles of 1562, the doctrines of the Church of England central to the evangelical tradition, Article XXVIII states:

> *The Sacrament of the Lord's Supper was not by Christ's ordinance reserved, carried about, lifted up, or worshipped.*

In the mid-nineteenth century, however, the Tractarians, the earliest manifestation of the Oxford Movement, gradually, and for the most part secretly, began to promote Reservation again.[2][3] According to Nigel Yates in his book *Anglican Ritualism in Victorian Britain 1830-1910:*

> *fewer than a dozen churches had begun to reserve the Blessed Sacrament in an aumbry or tabernacle before the 1890s. The first church to do so was St James the Less in Liverpool where it was reserved in a side chapel from 1875.*

St James the Less, the daughter church of St Martin-in-the-Fields in Liverpool, had been specially built in 1869 to the specifications of the vicar of St Martin's, Father Cecil Wray. Wray wanted the new church to accommodate the kind of elaborate Catholic ritual he was promoting in the city, including Reservation. St James the Less was George Chapman's first curacy. R.S., Chapman's biographer, puts the date of Reservation of the Sacrament at St James the Less even earlier than 1875.[4] Writing about the early years of Chapman's curacy there between 1869-73, she reports on the measures taken by the clergy during an epidemic:

> *It was found necessary to reserve the Blessed Sacrament, as there was often no time, and certainly no possibility of celebrating in the infected rooms. It was reserved in the Sister's Oratory, and many a night they were called up by the devoted priest (Chapman) who came for it to communicate some dying patient.*[5]

Arthur Wagner would have been aware of the tradition of Reservation at St James the Less, and indeed, this may well have been another contributing factor in his decision to import a curate from the other end of the country – precisely because George Chapman had experience of Reservation, and of dealing with the sectarian unrest that it was likely to engender.[6] (Protestant 'orange' opposition was strong in Liverpool). George Chapman arrived at the Annunciation on April 15th 1877. By November 1st he had opened a ward of the Confraternity of the Blessed Sacrament which promoted sacramental veneration.[7] It seems reasonable to suppose therefore that Father Chapman might have sought at this time to introduce the practice of Reservation (promoted by his mentoring priest in Liverpool, Cecil Wray) into his new church.[8]

The Real Presence

Transubstantiation became the second major issue of contention between the factions of the Church of England. The revised *Book of Common Prayer* of

1662 states in its Black Rubric:

> *It is hereby declared, that thereby no adoration is intended, or ought to be done, either unto the Sacramental Bread or Wine there bodily received, or unto any Corporal Presence of Christ's natural Flesh and Blood. For the Sacramental Bread and Wine remain still in their very natural substances, and therefore may not be adored; (for that were Idolatry, to be abhorred of all faithful Christians;) and the natural Body and Blood of our Saviour Christ are in Heaven, and not here; it being against the truth of Christ's natural Body to be at one time in more places than one.*

However, it is Roman Catholic belief, shared by Anglo-Catholics, that during the ceremony of the Eucharist, the bread and wine that are offered by the priest are miraculously transformed into the actual body and blood of Christ. In this way the communicant partakes of the incarnation, and Christ's real presence is revealed to and in that person. This is known as 'the Real Presence'. Though the majority of churches acknowledge Christ's special presence in the Eucharist, the Lutheran church for example, most Protestant and non-conformist traditions do not believe in the corporeal manifestation of Christ as Catholics do. They believe that, during the Eucharist, the communicant is symbolically participating in the consuming of Christ's body and blood, and this encourages His spiritual presence.

As a consequence of the Catholic belief in objective transubstantiation, the consecrated host could be reserved, outside the Mass, not only to administer to the sick and the dying, but also for veneration. And, indeed, in the 1870s and 1880s, this is what began to happen in a few Anglican churches inspired by the Oxford Movement, including the Annunciation. It was reserved either for the Exposition, when the Sacrament is displayed in a monstrance (usually of solar design) on the altar, allowing the faithful to pray before it, or for Benediction, when the priests prostrate themselves before the Sacrament before holding it aloft in the monstrance to bless the congregation. The Church of England meanwhile, officially remained implacably opposed to Reservation, except in extremis, and to the devotional practices associated with it.

The Annunciation has always revered the Real Presence in the Mass, and it has a tradition of practising Benediction. But when did the practice actually begin there? In her biography of Chapman, R.S. writes of her subject:

> *It is difficult to write with sufficient reverence of his intense love and deep devotion to the Presence of Jesus in the Blessed Sacrament of the altar. It was once said of him in Liverpool, 'To see Mr Chapman celebrate is better than*

any sermon on the Real Presence.' And it was even so. As one of his curates said, 'The prostrate form, the soul enraptured, burning with love, was a sight not soon to be forgotten.'

'The prostrate form' gives it away. This is unmistakably a description of Benediction, and it suggests that it was performed at the Annunciation. R.S. does not name the author of the remark (it is most likely Edwin Green) because of the sensitivity around the whole subject of adoration. Is it because these were necessarily secretive practices in Chapman's day? Why is neither Exposition or Benediction mentioned? To speak of them more openly would only have brought them to the attention of the sectarian Protestants groups and of the Diocese. Any Reservation, let alone Exposition of the Sacrament had to be performed clandestinely among Anglo-Catholics at this time.

Even as late as 1914 the issue was still contentious within the wider Church of England, and could not be spoken of openly. In the Jubilee Book produced for the Annunciation's fiftieth anniversary, Rocksborough Remington Smith (later Bishop of Ontario) looked back at Chapman's ministry, when he himself would have been a teenager. The passage is remarkably similar to the one quoted above.

Who of us, his spiritual children, will ever forget the intense reverence with which he celebrated the Holy Mysteries, so genuine that there was no need to argue with us about the truth of the Real Presence. We had felt it, we had experienced it, with a conviction that needed no external support.[10]

'Rocky' Smith could be describing Eucharist here, but his allusion to the controversy around the Real Presence suggests he may also be recalling Chapman's adoration of the exposed Sacrament. These descriptions are as close as their authors dared go in describing the 'illegal' practice of Benediction. Yet both writers felt they had a duty to describe these scenes to do justice to George Chapman's religion.

R.S., who would have witnessed these rites herself, also refers to the enthusiasm with which Father Chapman and the Sisters of Bethany greeted the creation of an oratory, the Chapel of the Transfiguration, out of part of the vestibule of the Annunciation, in 1886.[11] The oratory memorialised the form in which, according to the gospels, Jesus appeared to the disciples on a high mountain transformed into radiance, and speaking with Moses and Elijah. It was in this chapel that the Blessed Sacrament was to be reserved. The first Eucharist was celebrated there on August 6th that year. We are told that just before his death in 1891 George Chapman 'passed into the little oratory where the Blessed Sacrament was reserved for the dying'. It seems likely that he had indeed created the chapel specifically for the purpose of veneration, and modelled it on the idea of the oratory at St James the Less. Edwin Green, assistant priest at the Annunciation, tells us Father Chapman was praying before the Reserved Sacrament in this chapel at the hour of his death. Little did he know he had built the place of his own transfiguration.

We also know for certain that the practice of Benediction was already happening regularly [12] at the Annunciation by the time of Father Hinde's incumbency (1896-1910), as its prohibition was the explicit reason for his resignation (see Chapter 7). But the evidence suggests that both Reservation and Exposition were introduced by George Chapman quite early in his tenure at the Annunciation, and that Arthur Wagner may have encouraged him in these practices.[13] If this is so, in the context of Yates's research (where he gives the next earliest Reservation as St Margaret's Liverpool in 1878), it would make the Annunciation the second oldest church in the Church of England to reserve the Sacrament after the Reformation.[14] Because the dockland church of St James the Less was obliterated by German bombing in WWII, it would now also mean that the Annunciation qualifies as the oldest surviving Anglican church in which the Sacrament was reserved and Benediction performed.

6. GATHERING CLOUDS

W E HAVE NOW entered what might be described as the halcyon days of the Annunciation. In contrast to the ragged community that had been living around the original mission, the church was now at the centre of a bustling urban parish. In her biography of George Chapman, R.S. describes the area around the church (still not yet called Hanover) in 1893.

> *Fifty years ago there were only a few houses scattered here and there, among market gardens made on the side of what once formed part of the Brighton Downs. Now there are sixteen streets of small, modern houses for artisans; eight streets lie in parallel lines, intersected by an upward road; two streets are occupied by small shopkeepers of various trades. At 1pm the streets are thronged by men returning for their dinners... There are also a great number of small laundries. With the exception of the bottom row of houses facing the main road, which are of a somewhat superior kind, the whole parish is essentially poor.*

The Annunciation, as a focal point, played no small part in creating this community. But the description also gives us an idea of the needs that the church was now serving which had so exhausted its first vicar.

The sectarian atmosphere in Hanover remained relatively calm during the short incumbency of Chapman's successor, Father Reginald Fison. Liturgically, at the Bishop's request, Fison made few alterations.[1] But his pastoral style was rather more worldly than his predecessor. A former teacher who perhaps understood the attention span of his flock, he kept his sermons brief. 'Simplicity is the great thing,' he was fond of saying, 'just simplicity.' But, unlike his predecessor, who spoke extempore from notes, Father Fison was not a charismatic preacher. The simplicity could feel random, and the theme seldom strayed from that of sin. It was elsewhere that Fison's strengths lay, supporting the prayer-life of the church, encouraging the telling of the rosary, sitting for hours with his parishioners in their homes. It is said that he sat up all night with a drunkard to help him resist temptation. Quietly, too, he made innovations, introducing the Christmas Crib to make the Nativity more accessible to the children.

Father Fison was a social priest. On his arrival, he had expressed his surprise at the lack of social clubs within the church, and these were quickly organised, establishing a strong tradition of social activity at the Annunciation that has continued into the present day. The first clubs met in the Iron Room, (earlier known as 'Zoar', after one of the five cities of the plain of Jordan in Genesis) an oblong structure with a corrugated iron roof which had been erected in the school yard (now the garden of the Clergy House). Father Fison also enthusiastically supported several Annunciation cricket teams. The Senior Eleven was captained by Fison's assistant priest the Reverend J. Gatley. Fison himself occasionally turned out for the team, and looked forward to the day when a member of the church might be selected for the County.

In this nurturing and encouraging atmosphere, the clubbable Father Fison built on Father Chapman's legacy, and the congregation continued to grow, with 10,000 communions being registered for 1894, the peak of worship in the church's history. The remodelling of the building kept pace with the rising numbers. In 1892, Edmund Scott's partner W.T. Cawthorn added the tower and the Memorial Room, (in memory of Father Chapman) at the north-east corner.

Then on Boxing Day 1895, with the parish thriving, Father Fison was tragically struck down with typhoid fever, (a fate not uncommon in nineteenth-century Hanover). Once more, the parish was in mourning. Arthur Wagner felt he had to act quickly to keep up the momentum that Chapman and Fison had created. As Father Fison's successor he appointed a curate from St Bartholomew's the Reverend Henry Hinde. Father Hinde had been considered for the

Annunciation on the death of Father Chapman, but Wagner had opted for the more mild-mannered Fison, who had gained his pastoral experience ministering among the Devon poor. This time, Wagner did choose Hinde, and the decision was ultimately to demonstrate the wisdom of his original judgement.

Like Wagner, Henry Hinde came from an ecclesiastical background, and though he struggled with the pastoral demands of the new parish, he willingly embraced the ritual traditions that Father Chapman had instigated, and that Father Fison had augmented.[2] His liturgical extravagance, however, combined with a humourless manner, quickly revealed to his parishioners that he was not cut from the same ascetic cloth as his two predecessors. This may also account for the swift departure of Father Fison's previous curates, (one of them, Chapman's devoted assistant, Edwin Green[3]) and the appointment of two new ones, Fathers Pearce and Shebbeare.

Hinde was an intellectual theologian, whose sermons, in the understated words of his own successor, Father Carey, 'were sometimes a little beyond the intellectual reach of some of his hearers'. Carey goes on to say:

I expect it would be true to say that some people found him a little reserved at times. He was not always very forth-coming at first sight. He needed time to know people intimately. But there are those today who worship at the church who can never speak enthusiastically enough of his deep and overflowing kindness to them on all occasions, but especially in times of sickness.

According to Carey, Hinde had an extraordinary relationship to suffering, which he regarded as a salutary path to the understanding of Christ's own sufferings on our behalf. He was thus at his best as a priest when parishioners found themselves in extremis. He was also a fine administrator with a head for business, what he called his 'commercial instinct'. He raised the money and commissioned the building of the present Clergy House. It was dedicated to Father Fison's memory in 1898, (though the date on the foundation stone gives a year earlier).

Nevertheless, there is no doubt that, with Hinde's arrival, the tone of the parish changed. A testy and admonishing edge crept in to the monthly address to his flock in the Parish Magazine. The annual 'Treats' and suppers which Father Fison had encouraged, sat awkwardly with him. Only one (boys) cricket match is reported in the summer of 1896, and there was no question of Father Hinde himself ever doffing the biretta in favour of donning the pads. A zealous catechiser, a successful outing for him was judged in terms of the children's decorum, rather than their enjoyment; and he seems to have valued only the devotional content of any parish activity. To get a flavour of the man, here is his description of the 'Infant Treats' in the Parish Magazine:

> *This event, always an arduous undertaking for the teachers, was successfully brought off on Monday. A vast concourse of infants assembled in Church as usual after which they were carted in several wagons to a shady annexe of Preston Park. Here they disported themselves as the manner of infants is. It is sufficient to say that Fr. Green was in the company in order to make it known that both his and their happiness was supreme. After being safely conveyed back to the Schools, they were given a substantial tea, and sent home in a state of great complacency with regard to the day's proceedings.*

Hinde left the engagement with children to others, and if he was obliged to attend the 'Treats' and choir outings, he would be found wandering as an observer, preoccupied with his new-fangled Kodak, occasionally photographing the bemusing recreations unfolding before him.

Neither did Hinde demonstrate great commitment to the Annunciation Schools, offering no apparent resistance to the advancing secularization of education in his parish; though one might argue that his hands were tied by the civil legislation of the time.[4]

A curious entry stands out in the Parish Magazine, a year after Father Hinde's installation at the Annunciation:

> *A very handsome and valuable ring was given in one of the almsbags on Low Sunday at the High Mass. It is intended to have the jewels – a peridot and sixteen diamonds – set in the knob of one of the chalices.*

It is striking that such a rich gift intended as alms for the relief of the poor (in which Hanover still abounded), should be redirected to adorn an already golden chalice in the church. But that is a mark of Hinde's style, where everything was to be sacrificed to the adoration of the Sacrament, and where the parish itself, and its human needs were of lesser importance. Observing all this, Arthur Wagner, now reaching seventy, must have realised that Father Hinde's incumbency was bound to bring sectarian conflict in the parish to a head. And it did.

7. HENRY HINDE'S JOURNEY TO ROME

LTHOUGH THE FIRST and second vicars of the Annunciation had brought relative calm to the Annunciation, opposition to the Catholic Revival had not died down nationally. The ritualist controversy was further inflamed in 1897 by Walter Walsh's publication of a forensic study of Catholic Ritual within the Church of England entitled *The Secret History of the Oxford Movement*. Walsh collected information from all over the country, particularly on the 'clandestine activities' of the Society of the Holy Cross and the Confraternity of the Blessed Sacrament (a cell of which had been established at the Annunciation under Father Chapman twenty years earlier, as we have seen). The intention of Walsh's book was to foment public anger against idolatrous ritualistic practice in the Oxford Movement – the Reservation of the Sacrament for Exposition, the promotion of the doctrine of purgatory, the practice of praying for the dead, and the insistence on auricular confession to a priest. Walsh's book and its speedy reprinting in multiple editions give us some idea of how strong public feeling was still running against Catholic practice in Britain in the final decade of the nineteenth century.

Direct action against the Catholic Revival was now being coordinated nationally by one John Kensit. Kensit was a London bookseller, member of the

Church Association, and founder (in 1889) of the Protestant Truth Society, and the Wycliffe Preachers, an organization dedicated to the harassment of ritualistic clergy.

In 1898 the Archbishop of Canterbury declared the use of incense and portable lights within the service illegal. Typically, the Annunciation was one of the churches that refused to comply with the ban. Learning of this disobedience, Kensit arranged for his friend, George Davey, to take up residence in Lincoln Cottages, so that he might join the Annunciation's electoral roll. Thus legitimised, in 1899, Davey then took legal proceedings against Father Hinde and the churchwardens under the new law in the Consistory Court of the Archdeaconry of Lewes, seeking a faculty to remove 'ornaments' from the church. The faculty was granted, and though Hinde and the churchwardens appealed to the High Court, their appeal was rejected. Still there was no compliance, the church preferring to follow a line of passive resistance. In 1900, Father Hinde observed to the members of the Confraternity of the Blessed Sacrament, (of which he was 'the Superior'), that:

> the recent attacks on the doctrine and ceremonial of the church appear to have roused people to increased earnestness and devotion. The Blessed Sacrament has been the chief object of attack, and we note with thankfulness in the Parish an increase in devotion to the Blessed Sacrament especially on the part of members of the Confraternity.

He urged the latter to pray 'that the recent opinions of the Archbishops of Canterbury and York may be over-ruled for the good of the Church'. But they were not. Father Hinde's ministry at the Annunciation soon became the focus of renewed attacks from the Protestant opposition. In 1900, John Kensit himself moved to Brighton and stood as an 'Independent Conservative' in the general election. We can gauge the strength of Protestant sectarian feeling in the town by the fact that, basing his campaign on the single issue of curbing ritualism, Kensit polled 4693 votes. Services at the Annunciation were now frequently disrupted by the Protestants, but the congregation, especially the younger members, did not take it lying down. 'Onlooker' reports in the Centenary Booklet:

> When Father Hinde was vicar we suffered from the attention of the Kensitites. If they thought the Annunciation would be easy prey they were disappointed. I can remember Mr Wood taking them out during a commotion during Mass and we choirboys were itching to get out and at them. Our support of the 'little church' earned us the name of 'the Annunciation hooligans' in the press but that did not stop us and I remember one of the choirboys clinging to Mr Kensit's whiskers.

There may be some false memory here. There's no documentation (except 'Onlooker') that Kensit ever set foot in the church, let alone attempted to disrupt it himself. He had once promised 'a thousand riots in a thousand churches' up and down the country, but it seems unlikely he would have risked public exposure in one as partisan as the Annunciation. Whether this was Kensit himself, George Davey, or simply 'a Kensitite' is moot; what is significant is the fact that there was no pacifism in the face of the attacks, but rather militant defiance. This too was the tenor of Father Hinde's attitude towards the Bishop's Palace in Chichester.

In August 1902 a faculty was issued by the bishop, Ernest Wilberforce (grandson of William) to remove any items of an idolatrous nature. Again, Father Hinde ignored the law. The Annunciation stood firm, and it was not until a year later, that George Davey and his associates entered the church and, carefully, with the appropriate tools, removed the offending items. The expropriation was condoned by the local constabulary, which posted a constable at either end of Washington Street, and stationed a further back-up force in Southover Street. Contrary to popular lore, on this occasion, the small congregation present did not attempt to resist the kidnappers. Davey, who was also accompanied by a solicitor and a press reporter, calmly wrapped the artefacts and placed them in a waiting van. They were then taken to his accommodation in Lincoln Cottages where they were photographed. This photo was swiftly printed and distributed as a postcard, to offer proof to the public of Hinde's flouting of the law.

Looking at the postcard, one can still recognise some of the statuary – the statue of the Blessed Virgin of course, the Annunciation's most revered figure in the nave, and also a statue of Joseph, which still stands in the sacristy of the church today. Significant also, amongst the candlesticks and monstrances, there is a rudimentary tabernacle, further evidence of the Reservation of the Sacrament, one of the main Protestant bugbears.

Hinde was not unprepared for what he saw as sacrilege. His successor Father William Carey describes his demeanour at the time:

> *Those who remember those days are agreed that Father Hinde showed the most perfect self-control and restraint. He was most dignified, and kept his head splendidly. There was no shrieking – no hysterics. He was as dignified and patient in his bearing as was a greater than he – the great Athanasius himself – under a storm of obloquy and persecution. As an old member of the congregation described it to me: 'It was then that he shone.'*

Perhaps Father Hinde remained calm because he had already discovered that, in common law, although Davey had the right to remove the items, he had no right to keep them. The churchwardens made a petition to the courts to this effect. This time the ruling was given in the Annunciation's favour, and the items were returned within a week, although not put on display again for some years. The author Herbert Hamilton Maughan, writing in the 1920s, records that a large number of the congregation went to retrieve the kidnapped artefacts from Lincoln Cottages, and carried them back to the Clergy House singing lustily 'Faith Of Our Fathers'. This may be a later embroidery on the story.

The contentious statue of The Blessed Virgin Mary, which still stands at the front of the nave today, had been raised only a few years earlier as a memorial to Father Fison.[1] It was the largest object to be removed from the Church by its Protestant opponents. In recent years, a statue of the Blessed Virgin, somewhat lighter than the expropriated one, has been proudly paraded through the streets by the congregation on Hanover Day, without opposition.

At the time of these events, John Kensit was already dead, killed by a chisel thrown at his head during a religious demonstration in Liverpool. Father Wagner had also died the previous year and was thus, mercifully, spared the sacrilegious attack on the little church he had founded.

Yet the 'kidnapping' episode only seemed to steel Hinde's resolve. After the troubles in 1903, he wrote:

> The attempts recently made by Bishops to abolish the practice of reserving the Blessed Sacrament had proved futile, and they were now directed against any reverence or devotion being paid to It. This should be an additional incentive to us to render to our Lord the loving honour and worship which is at all times due to Him. The recent grievous sacrilege in our own Church also called for repeated acts of reparation and increase devotion. It was satisfactory to notice that the Thursday Exposition was more largely attended both by CBS associates and others.

Hinde was already anticipating the next stage of the battle – this time precisely over Exposition – that is, the exposure of the Reserved Sacrament and the performance of Benediction before it. In 1910, Wilberforce's successor as Bishop of Chichester, Charles Ridgeway, outlawed this practice in the Diocese. When the ruling was challenged by the Anglo-Catholic lobby, Ridgeway offered the clarification that 'the Reserved Sacrament shall be kept for its primitive and Catholic use – namely, for the sick and the dying, and that it shall not be used at any public services, such as Exposition or Benediction'. But this was anathema to Hinde. He, along with two curates from the Annunciation, Fathers Henry Rhodes Prince and Ernest Shebbeare, together with the Vicar of St Bartholomew's, A.R.C. Cocks, no longer felt they could be obedient to the Bishop's authority.

This precipitated what *The Sussex Daily News* described as 'the Brighton church crisis'. The newspaper anticipated that Hinde and Cocks would reconsider their resignation, but after a tetchy exchange of letters between Bishop Ridgeway and the Reverend Cocks in *The Times*, and despite fervent appeals from the congregations of the Annunciation and St Bartholomew's, on the 12th September 1910, following Cocks' example, Hinde formally departed the Church of England and went across to Rome. The recusant priests were welcomed with open arms. *The Tablet*, the Catholic newspaper, immediately offered its warmest congratulations. It also reprinted a report of Hinde's farewell sermon, unsurprisingly on the theme of suffering, from *The Sussex Daily News*:

> *His voice rang out thrillingly when he declared that the doctrine of the Real Presence was far more precious to him than all the world could give or take away. If they had to suffer for it, let them bear their sufferings for the Master's sake, doing all to His glory, but never let them surrender their faith in this glorious heritage of the Catholic Church.*

News of the clergymen's departure resounded around the world, with *The Adelaide Advertiser* observing, 'The Roman Catholic organs, it is interesting to note, devote more attention to the question than they usually bestow upon an Anglican controversy'. Closer to home, *The Guardian* described the group of clergy as belonging 'to the worthy, but peculiarly trying, company of good men who are impracticable'.

Hinde and his curates' defection was a devastating blow to the Annunciation. 'A dark cloud hangs over St. Bartholomew's,' wrote *The Tablet*, 'and even darker is the sorrow which has fallen on the people of the Annunciation'.[2] Documentation of this rift has all but vanished from the church. Only one notice has survived purgation, tucked away in the Vestry Minutes Book, expressing the mood at the time. It is a scratchy entry for Easter 1911, noting the passing of the following resolution:

> *This vestry desires to place on record its deep grief at the departure of the late Vicar and its very great appreciation of his past devoted service to the cause of Christ in this parish, whilst regretting his severance from the Church of England.*

The length of Father Chapman and Father Hinde's tenure was roughly the same, and yet their outcome was vastly different. If anything, George Chapman was working in a more hostile environment nationally, and yet he had been able to steer the ship into calm waters. From the outset, Henry Hinde's approach was uncompromising and confrontational towards those who did not share his belief. The attitude towards the Catholic Revival was already softening towards the end of his incumbency. In 1906, a Royal Commission effectively nullified the Public Worship Act by concluding more pluralism in public worship should be accepted. Had he remained inside the Church of England, Hinde would even have seen a blind eye being turned to Benediction. It remained a regular feature of worship at the Annunciation for many years, up to Father Bullivant's time, and it is still occasionally performed in the church today. But ultimately, it was almost as if Father Hinde welcomed the sectarian opposition, because it gave him the opportunity to defend the Sacrament and eventually to martyr himself publicly in their cause by resigning from the Church of England.

Hinde was received into the Catholic Church by the Bishop of Southwark, and thereafter studied for the priesthood at the Accademia dei Nobili Ecclesiastici in Rome. He was ordained in Rome by Cardinal Merry del Val in June 1911[3] and became a Privy Chamberlain in 1915, the year of his appointment to the charge of St. Vincent's in Clapham. During his Roman training, however, Hinde had returned to Brighton where he was attached for a time to St Joseph's Roman Catholic Church, neighbouring the parish of the Annunciation. This probably accounts for the story, much-loved locally, that he took the Annunciation's statue of Joseph with him to St Joseph's when he left the church.[4] The story is most likely apocryphal. What Hinde did take with him to Rome and away from the Annunciation was approximately half of the existing congregation.

Whether these parishioners crossed to Rome or to other Anglican churches, it is now hard to ascertain. Some members of the congregation, it would not be hard to imagine, witnessing such internecine strife in the Christian fellowship, may have given up on the church altogether.

Monsignor Hinde, as he became, devoted much of the rest of his life to setting up a 'clearing house' in the Midlands for the reception of priests crossing to Rome, where they might be re-trained as Roman Catholics. In 1919 Hinde had an audience with the pope who was 'favourable to the idea'.[5] Monsignor Hinde died in 1922 at the age of sixty-six. There is very little record of his incumbency left in the church. It is as if he has been airbrushed from its history.

The original mission 1864

The gas-lit mission before the expansion. Note the original Stations of the Cross and the inscribed rafters

Arthur Douglas Wagner

Richard Durnford Bishop of Chichester who
preached at the consecration of the church 1884

John Mason Neale

Father George Chapman
First Vicar

Aubrey Beardsley as a youth

The Mysterious Rose Garden
or 'The Annunciation'

Beardsley as a
young man

Reginald Fison
Second Vicar

Henry Hinde (centre) Third Vicar
with his curates

Group of Idols and other Objects condemned as illegal and removed from the Church of the Annunciation, Brighton, Sept. 1st 1903

The kidnapped 'idols'. Note the tabernacle on the left

Rev. Wagner in later life

Charles Ridgeway Bishop of Chichester at the
time of Henry Hinde's defection

Walter Greed

William Carey
Fourth Vicar

The exterior of the church showing the Clergy House opened in 1898

John Tiley
Fifth Vicar

Geoffrey Davis
Sixth Vicar

Father Clarabut with the scout troop outside 'Zoar', the Iron Room, in the 1920s

8. THE GREAT WAR

THE DISUNITY brought about by Henry Hinde's departure for Rome should not be underestimated; and yet this adversity seems to have brought in wider support from far beyond the parish.[1] As Father William Carey, the new incumbent put it in the Statement of Accounts for 1911:

> There is no Church in the land, I should imagine, which has warmer friends than the Annunciation. If it were not so we must have gone under financially during the past year. As it is we have kept going. In January 1911 I made an appeal for money in the Church Times. About £80 came in response. This put us out of debt and gave us a good and fresh start.

Carey established the 'Farthing Fund' in 1912, whereby his parishioners might put aside their smallest coins for the benefit of the church. This practice has now survived for over a century. Carey was thus a practical man who went about his work in the community in a very different way from his predecessor. Consequently, the sectarian problems which had bedevilled the church once again receded, and for a few years William Carey patiently rebuilt the congregation back up to a reasonable level. Even he could not have foreseen the next crisis by which the Church would be engulfed, however, because it was an international one.

The Great War began in August 1914. 'It came with a tremendous shock', Carey wrote, 'Too bad to be true…an outrage on reason and sanity.' The tone of the vicar's first wartime message was nationalistic: 'May Almighty God vindicate our cause and that of our Allies,' and there was no question where the blame for the causation of the war lay: 'A bully in the last resort must be faced.' But William Carey was not a warmonger. He acknowledged that during the Boer War:

> we bragged and laughed in our foolish pride of imperial power; today there is no voice of arrogance, no "frantic boast", nor blasphemous "trust in reeking tube and iron shard".

The vicar is quoting from Kipling's poem *Recessional* (from which the line 'Lest We Forget' is drawn), and, together with the poet, he is counselling against jingoism. Yet there was no hint of pacifism either in his attitude to the Great War. It was informed by 'a great desire to stand by the weak'. Very soon most of the able-bodied men of his parish had heeded his message and volunteered.

The planned fiftieth anniversary celebrations of the church, which fell in that very month of August 1914, had to be toned down. Nevertheless the Jubilee Number of the Parish Magazine was printed and sold for sixpence, or a shilling bound, and was deemed a great success. It was favourably reviewed in the *The Brighton Herald*:

> It is said that a building set upon a hill cannot be hid. This may not be strictly true of the Church of the Annunciation, which though set upon a hillside, is hidden away in one of the most densely populated districts in Brighton; but all the poor and lowly folk in the neighbourhood know it as a source from which there flows a neverfailing flow of spiritual comfort – ay, and of material helpfulness in time of utmost need. The priests of the Annunciation have ever been the true and revered friends of the people.

The article reveals not only how populous Hanover had become by this time, but also how, in the adversity of the war, a new sense of community had began to grow up around the church, very different from the ideological struggles of the previous fifty years. Father Carey was not slow to identify the bonding nature of war and its galvanising effect on religious observance: 'Yet even in its horrors are born things of great worth,' he wrote '- a sense of dependence on God.' The frivolous, however, would necessarily have to be temporarily sacrificed to accommodate the earnest preoccupations of war. 'I give notice,' Carey alerted the congregation in the September issue of the Parish Magazine, 'that Miss Bird's Monday Dancing Class will not meet this side of Christmas'. By which time, presumably, as was popularly supposed, it would all be over.

By January 1915, the church was very much on a war footing. Even one of the churchwardens, Jim Medhurst (who was to play a key role at the Annunciation in the years to come), not the fittest of men, volunteered and was quickly promoted to Sergeant in the Egyptian Expeditionary Force. In response to a national appeal by the Archbishop of Canterbury and Lord Kitchener, a War Abstinence Society was formed at the Annunciation, to replace the dwindling Temperance Society at the church and to encourage sobriety. Though the men of the parish were setting off for the war, some to postings in quite exotic locations in Egypt, Palestine and India, movement was restricted for the rest of the parish. The congregation were unable to attend the ordination of their deacon, the highly popular Father Clarabut, as fully-fledged priest, because it would have meant travelling all the way to Eastbourne.

The vicar wrote in the Parish Magazine:

> *Our choir dwindles steadily, at least the men part of it. Only three left, I think, and two over military age. It spoils the singing, of course; but I don't regret it, rather I boast of it. One after another they disappear, to reappear for a brief moment in khaki. And how well they look in it; what military bearing; what patriotic pride shines in their eyes. How proud we all are of them!*

Carey regularly published letters from the Annunciation's servicemen in the Parish Magazine, initially received from their training units, and then from the theatres of war to which they were despatched. The sense of bonding the men felt with the church is evident in many of the letters. George Cripps, a regular correspondent, wrote from France:

> *Of course, I can't tell you where we are, but we have shifted nearer to the trenches within the next few days. The other night we had to turn out, and marched nine miles to a place the Germans have been shelling. They seem to have made a mark of the Cathedral there... I have not seen anything of Chris Button* (another Annunciation correspondent) *since I have been out here, but I think he is twelve miles further down the line...I received the February Magazine yesterday and was pleased at the number of letters from different fellows...*

Because of the rigorous censorship of the letters, they contain little of the horrors of the trenches, with few details of the actual fighting; but they are poignant nonetheless. Throughout the spring of 1915 Harry Rolfe, a server of the church, with aspirations of ordination and missionary work in Africa, corresponded with updates of his progress down to the Mediterranean with the Royal Naval Division:

> *They have given me two suits of khaki and sand shoes – we are being rigged out very quickly... We shall probably land at Malta first, before going on to the fighting. You would like to see me in my helmet (I look a nut in it!) We have had a very rough time of it these last days... So we are now once more in the Danger Zone. Last night they saw a submarine. Still we are safe so far...*

In the same issue of the magazine in which the last extract from his 'diary' was published, the late news was appended that Harry Rolfe had been killed in action. Able Seaman Rolfe was killed 'in a charge' within days of arriving in the Dardanelles. He had been pitched straight into the disastrous third battle of Krithia. The first wave of the Royal Naval Division's advance managed to reach and capture the Ottoman trenches. When the second wave—the Collingwood Battalion in which Rolfe was serving—attempted to continue the advance, 'they were caught in enfilade fire from the right where the French advance had failed'. The battalion, which comprised exclusively newly arrived reinforcements, was utterly annihilated and never reformed.

One parishioner, Private P. Nicholl of the 13th Royal Sussex Regiment, was decorated for conspicuous gallantry, and in this case, we do have a full account of his deeds.

> *During the whole of the battle the only means of communication other than pigeon was by runner, and the enemy shelling was unusually intense in this battle, rendering communication a most difficult and dangerous task. Despite this, on every occasion Pte. Nicholl responded with utmost readiness. Early in the engagement one of the dugouts occupied by Batt. H.Q. runners, was blown in by shell fire, and several were killed or wounded. Pte. Nicholl was blown some distance into water and completely saturated. Despite this he reported for duty, and proceeded to the front line with messages, and carried on until the Battalion was relieved.*

In July 1917, the Riddles family tragically lost two sons in a matters of weeks. Reggie Riddles, a sixteen-year-old year old server at the church, was blown up with HMS Vanguard, when over 800 men were lost in an accidental explosion in Scapa Flow. The following March, his nineteen-year-old elder brother James died of his wounds with the Royal Sussex Regiment on the Italian Front. Their father, Corporal Arthur Riddles, survived the war.

Alongside its letters from the front, the Parish Magazine also carried some trenchant propaganda. The following diatribe, communicated through the assistant priest, Father Mainwaring, and published in June 1915, when national morale was flagging, is a significant example.

*The war is not going on as it should, and the people of England are dreadfully to blame. The apathy, indifference, and levity of people in England makes the hearts of us who are out here feel sick – one feels as if one was being stabbed in the back all the time, as if one's worst enemies are one's own people. It's awful! The Derby, and Ascot, and strikes and drink at home; bullets, shells, and poison gas here! Does **nobody** realise we are fighting for our very national existence against a vast, powerful, scientific, determined, unscrupulous people who will stick at nothing to crush us. A nation which has been preparing and planning for war for years, a nation every man, woman and child of whom is working, fighting to get us under their heel.'*

With hindsight, it is easy to see the pen that wrote these words being wielded in Whitehall, rather than at the Front, but their publication in the Annunciation Parish Magazine demonstrates the militant patriotism with which even members of the local clergy approached the war. In November 1915 Father Carey went so far as to organise a 'recruiting march' around the streets of Hanover to encourage local children to join the Sunday School. The military-style parade brought in 40 new members. Clearly, there was no place for pacifism in the parish.

Throughout the war, Carey encouraged as much community activity as possible. The men's club often wanted for members, so many being overseas, but, as well as the regular Sunday Schools, Carey oversaw thriving Girls and Boys Clubs, a Band of Hope for Boys and Girls, Mothers Meetings, Boy Scouts, a Girls Guild, and even a Parish Entertainment Committee. One wonders what Father Hinde would have made of this. (Perhaps it was fortunate after all he was not in charge of the Annunciation in wartime). The accounts reveal the church even paid for swimwear for the children in the exceptionally hot summers.

One of the last casualties of the war among the Annunciation congregation was Walter Greed. Born in 1885, he had lived with his family at 25 Washington Street. Known as 'Wall' or 'Wally', he had attended the Annunciation Schools, and was catechised at the church and confirmed (at St Bartholomew's) on 12th December 1897. This event was recorded in the family Bible. He must have had a talent for music, as he found employment as a piano tuner. This took him to Aldershot. The census shows him working for the Music Warehouse there in 1911. In a garrison town, it was a short step to the recruiting barracks, and he duly signed up for the Royal Engineers at the outbreak of war, becoming a member of the 221st Army Troops Company. He survived right up until the spring of 1918, when his company was caught up in the massive German offensive around St Quentin and Bapaume, while retreating over the ground gained by the Allies during the Battle of the Somme of 1916. Launched from the Hindenburg Line, the offensive began on March 21st 1918.[2] Walter was reported missing on March 22nd, the second day of the offensive. His body was never recovered. His parents wrote in the family Bible: 'Loved by us, mourned by us, gone but never forgotten.'

Forty names were included on the Roll of Honour Carey commissioned in 1918. This still hangs by the War Altar in the south aisle of the church, the tabernacle of which is also inscribed in memory of the fallen of World War I. Amidst the slaughter and loss, there was a renewed sense of the fellowship that had been lost from the church over the Hinde affair. The common suffering of the war had found a focus at the Annunciation and bonded the whole community. Attendance had risen again, and for the first time since its foundation, one has the sense that the church had become the true heart of Hanover.

9. JEZEBEL, JEZEBEL!

WILLIAM CAREY used his first sermon after the signing of the Armistice to discuss unity among Christians. He acknowledged the differences in the Church of England over the sacraments:

Religious agreement with all Christian men, is out of our power to reach; courtesy, tolerance and gentleness we can at least cultivate.

In the Jubilee magazine of 1914 he had written of his vision for the Annunciation, which could serve as a mission statement for the church even today:

We have got to combine Services of gorgeousness of ceremonial on the one hand, with Services of the utmost simplicity and homeliness on the other. In a word, we have got to have "Roman" Elaborateness and "Dissenting" simplicity. The truth being, of course, that we must not make a present to Rome of all the beauty and stateliness of ceremonial; nor a present to Dissent of simplicity and naturalness.

In one sense, Carey's vision here is simply a continuation of Father Chapman's vision for the church. But Carey is writing with the schism Henry Hinde created still fresh in his mind, and he is outlining the case for an Anglo-

Catholic parish distinct from Rome, and well accommodated inside the Church of England. He goes on:

The English Church must cease to be prim and starchy; she must show herself elastic, and able to respond to the needs of those who love an elaborate ceremonial, and those who like homeliness and simplicity.

Carey was a caring priest and a cohesive force in the community. In him we begin to identify a more liberal strain of Catholicism at the Annunciation, which still continues in the congregation today. It was Carey who first identified one of the great qualities of the Annunciation: homeliness, what he calls elsewhere its 'Homeyness'. It was what so many of the letters from the Front yearned for, and to which most, but not all the letter-writers, returned with such joy, to resume their places as servers, sidesmen and in the choir.

William Carey, not much regarded by previous writers, was a great force for good at the Annunciation, skilfully guiding it beyond its clerical desertion, through the Great War and into calmer waters. It was his manner and his judgement that allowed homeliness to prosper again after the ideological severity of Father Hinde's tenure.

Carey resigned in 1924 to take over the vacancy at St Paul's, Brighton. He was replaced by Father J.C.G Tiley. With the success of the Anglo-Catholic Congress in Brighton in 1922, the liturgical practices that had been pioneered at the Annunciation had become more accepted in other churches. Brighton religion had now begun to be dominated by Anglo-Catholicism, which even became popularly known as 'the London Brighton and South Coast Religion'. Inspired by this popular endorsement, John Tiley had great ambitions for the visual and ceremonial development of the church. He set about its embellishment with gusto, commissioning many of the baroque elements that we see today.

Most notably, he remodelled the sanctuary, moving the choir to the organ chapel from its traditional place between the High Altar and the chancel screen. The sanctuary was then extended to its present form, and the screen removed and replaced by altar rails. The crucified Christ on the Vine and its two attendant figures, St Mary and St John, were also put in place as the rood at this time. The centre-piece of this remodelling, however, was the reredos behind the altar. Although Tiley's re-ordering of the sanctuary was mostly successful, it did undoubtedly compromise the beauty of the Burne-Jones window. I will discuss the artistic merits of the reredos and the rood in Appendix 2.

Despite the General Strike and the Depression, Hanover too, with no little thanks to the church, was slowly beginning to emerge from abject poverty and squalor. Perhaps because of his flamboyant taste, Father Tiley proved popular. The years of his incumbency, the late Twenties and early Thirties, produced a surprisingly settled period at the church, during which the congregational numbers continued to climb back towards the Victorian levels of the Chapman and Fison era.

So we should not imagine by any means that the life of the church in Hanover was always dominated by theological argument and sectarian division, or even that the majority were concerned with them. For most of the parishioners it was the daily activity of the church that provided the focus, and not just the *Kalendar*, the weekly timetable of services, offices and prayer intentions. Under successive vicars, beginning with Fison, social committees had been convened to organise outings, sports fixtures, pilgrimages, nativity tableaux for the congregation. The church acted as a community association might today. It provided a satisfying rhythm to parish life, and kept entertainment affordable. The church was open, for private prayer, for floral decoration, or even just to view the remarkable stained glass or Martin Travers' newly designed altar and reredos. Once a year, in August, the parish priest would sit in the church porch to receive voluntary contributions (above and beyond what was received in the plate on Sundays) for the upkeep of the church. It is a custom that seemed to lean on something much more ancient, perhaps even feudal and Italian. (It did not die out until the 1980s.) It conjures up a contented scene, on a hot August afternoon, with the children playing in Washington Street, the vicar conversing with his parishioners, and the occasional clink of a heavy half-crown dropping into the black leather almsbag. This too is the history of the Annunciation, and the better part of it.

10. DECLINE

AFTER TEN YEARS, Father Tiley followed in Carey's footsteps to take over at St Paul's. His own successor was a young idealistic Catholic and railway enthusiast, Father Geoffrey Davis, who favoured the Roman Mass, and, most notably, reintroduced elements of the Tridentine Latin into the Eucharist. But Davis was never to enjoy the best of health. After only three years in office, he died at Candlemas in 1937, aged 38. Lloyd Morrell, later Bishop of Lewes, wrote in tribute to him:

> *When he came to Brighton his health had already become less robust and the many hills which confront the parish priest of the Annunciation, did his heart no good. He never spared himself. He threw himself wholeheartedly into the life and tradition which he inherited from his distinguished predecessors... Shortly after Father Davis came to the Annunciation I followed him to Brighton... and therefore had the privilege of seeing at first hand the great contribution which God enabled him to make, in a few short years, to the history of this famous church... It so chanced that Bishop Bell and I came into church together for Fr. Davis' requiem. We stood for a moment looking at the catafalque and then the Bishop turned to me and said :- 'A great priest'.*

Once again the hill of Hanover and the rigours of the parish had tested the constitution of a relatively young Annunciation priest beyond its limits.

It was at this juncture that further sectarian troubles broke out at the Annunciation in which Bishop George Bell, now Bishop of Chichester, just like his predecessors, was to become inveigled. In February 1937, a month after Davis's death, as is customary at the beginning of an interregnum, the Parochial Church Council was asked to send their requirements to the 'Patron of the Benefice', that is: the Wagner Trustees, regarding his successor. The P.C.C. sent in two resolutions – firstly that the new priest should be celibate, and secondly that he would be 'prepared to continue the Catholic teaching and practice as has been from the inception of this Parish'. By March the new priest had been chosen, having presumably been interviewed by the Trustees. He was named as Father Paul Raybould, a staunch Anglo-Catholic. He had previously been a curate at St Martin's, Brighton, and was known to many at the Annunciation for his work with the local Sea Cadets. In the minute book for March 31st 1937, the P.C.C. Secretary is asked to write a letter of welcome to Father Raybould as their new parish priest. Though it is not recorded, his name must then have gone forward to the Diocese for approval. But was this letter ever sent? At their next meeting on May 21st, a discussion arose in the P.C.C. as to the nature of the welcoming reception to be given Father Raybould at his installation, which was planned for July 1st.

That event never took place. In the Finance Committee Minute Book for July 10th, Father Power is suddenly described as Vicar designate. The minute book of the P.C.C. records on August 11th: 'it was decided that an informal meeting with refreshments should be held in the church hall immediately after the institution of Father Power, to extend to him a hearty welcome'. Father Power was a curate at St Bartholomew's, and well-known to the locality, but he also suffered from ill-health, and seems an unlikely candidate to succeed Father Davis. There is no explanation of this parochial *volte face* during the summer of 1937. Father Raybould went on to serve as parish priest in East Anglia (where he established a parish church dedicated to Julian of Norwich). So it is unlikely there was any question of infirmity or scandal, and much more likely that the Diocese objected to the choice of the Wagner Trustees. It is a mystery which the present writer would wish to have solved, but once again, a page has been carefully excised from the minute book for that August meeting which might have revealed the answer.

We are perhaps given a clue to the stormy transition in a brief description of Father Power's chequered ministry, given in the Centenary Year book of 1964 by SS.B., one of Sisters of Bethany attached to the Annunciation.

> the Bishop, not approving of all that was done at the Annunciation, insisted on several alterations.

John Hawes, writing in his pamphlet *Ritual and Riot*, goes further:

> *the bishop decided his* (Davis's) *successor should comply with The Book of Common Prayer a little more.*

It is entirely possible that George Bell, the Bishop of Chichester, may have wished to have a more pliable incumbent at the Annunciation, who might bring the church more into the mainstream of the Church of England, rather than leading it ever closer towards Rome. Did he veto Father Raybould's appointment? This suspicion is raised because Father Power soon attempted to introduce *The Book of Common Prayer* (more associated with evangelical protestant liturgy) into the church, probably at the request of Bishop Bell. This was anathema to the church's tradition, so unpopular in fact that one of the Annunciation's curates, Father Hrada, disrupted High Mass for several months by calling out 'Jezebel! Jezebel!' whenever the prayerbook was used. He was eventually appeased by being allowed to continue to say the contentious sections of the Tridentine Mass in the Holy Name Chapel, while Father Power simultaneously conducted his common prayerful version in the main body of the church.

Neither should we think that the physical threat posed to the Annunciation had been left behind in the days of Father Hinde. This was the decade of the Biff Boys, of Moseley and William Joyce (both locally active), and of the British Union of Fascists whose sympathies were profoundly Protestant and who often rallied in Brighton. Extremist mobs were not uncommon, and street violence was in the air, even in Hanover. The churchwardens made sure that there were always some strong arms in every service. The choirboys were instructed to keep on singing whatever disturbance was taking place at the back of the church. Any protesters were efficiently removed by the two burly policemen who were regular members of the congregation, deliberately seated at the back of the church in case of trouble.

In the political pressure cooker of the late Thirties, the sectarian strife that had dogged the church's early days threatened to escalate in a new wave of nationalism. Once again it was the war that came to the rescue, when ideological differences were set aside in the face of a greater enemy. But WWII impacted the Annunciation with far less ferocity than the First. This is partly because the congregation itself had dwindled under Power to about forty regulars. One might have expected that the community bonding WWI had brought to the church might have been repeated. But the opposite was the case. Was it the disillusionment with a priest imposed by the bishop that drove many of the congregation away at this time? Or was it simply Power's lacklustre style? Even the most charitable observer, SS.B, remembers the seventh vicar as a peripheral and slightly comical figure from a bygone era:

> *Through it all moved an ageing figure in failing health. As one of the Sunday school children once said to him:- Father your hair is made of cotton wool! – ...and as he passed through the streets in his old-fashioned clerical hat, people have been known to remark:- 'Why there goes Mr Noah!'*

If the Diocese had put him up as a man of straw, hoping to wind down the church in order to close it, they were initially successful. The elderly priest was unable to hold the communion together. Many departed to rejoin their old vicar Father Tiley at St Paul's.[1] As the numbers fell away, so did the energy of the parish.

In 1939, however, Power did oversee the building of the Mission House in Lincoln Street, a purpose-built home for the Sisters of Bethany, who had been living in various cramped houses in the parish since their arrival in 1882.[2] This project was inherited from Father Tiley, and it is to him that some of the credit for the planning must go; but Father Power invested prodigious energy in actually getting the Mission House built. The opening, attended by Bishop Rocksborough Smith and Hugh Hordern, the Bishop of Lewes, was the high point of his incumbency.

Edwin Power's lowest ebb came in 1942. That year, his last assistant priest, Father Henry, deserted him. Power had begun his ministry at the Annunciation with five. 'It seems that for financial and other reasons, I must carry on single-handed for the present', he wrote in June of that year. Unlike during WWI, when the church had become the rallying-point of the community, the volunteers on which it has always depended had also begun to disappear:

> *The Cubs for the present will not meet. At the moment I do not know anyone to run the Pack. I suppose it is one result of the war, when all young men and women are being called up and almost all are engaged on war work in one form or another, that there should be a shortage of people able to undertake work for the church.*

Power was not cut from the same revivalist cloth as his predecessors at the Annunciation. The expedient circumstances of his appointment, his age and frailty, even a certain lack of charisma, all worked against his ministry. He had perhaps been too elderly and too infirm to take on the role in the first place. If he had been the compromise candidate, between the Bishop and the Annunciation, then that compromise now seemed misguided. By appointing

Father Power and taking the ideological Catholic heart out of the church the Bishop (if it was indeed he who made the decision) had inadvertently sapped its life-blood. During and after the Blitz, and for the rest of the war, Evensong was heard by a handful of worshippers in darkness, because of the blackout regulations. It is an apposite image for the state of the church at that time.

Father Power survived the war, deserted eventually even by his ailing housekeeper. But towards the end of his tenure, there was still some fight left in him and in the church he led. In June 1950, 'to save manpower and funds', a Diocesan Re-organisation Commission was announced. This initially proposed that the Annunciation should be amalgamated with the larger parish of St Martin's. The Annunciation's P.C.C. swiftly formed a special committee to fight the merger, led by Father Power. A detailed response was composed to the Diocese detailing the church's objections to the plan that July.[3] If the amalgamation were unavoidable, the P.C.C. were adamant that they wanted the church to be merged with St Bartholomew's, with which the Annunciation had greater traditional connections (even though St Martin's was also a Wagner church). The objections were read out from the pulpit at a Sunday Mass in August in place of the sermon. Eventually, a parochial deputation, including Father Power, was despatched from the church to the Bishop to voice their concerns. Thereafter, for a period of over two years, the issue lay in the long grass of Diocesan consultation.

Father Power did not to live to see the outcome. In May 1952, he was dismayed to be informed that the last two Sisters of Bethany were being withdrawn from the Mission House he had opened for them only thirteen years earlier. It was the coup de grâce. He died barely a month later, still in office, having hung on for over fifteen years, the longest incumbency at the Annunciation up to that point. This at least suggests a certain doggedness in his character; but it cannot be denied that these were essentially fifteen years of decline. By the opening of the Fifties, with its troubled history, and its diminished communion, from the Diocesan perspective, the Annunciation looked ripe for amalgamation, or even closure.

11. ROCKY

I T IS A TRADITIONAL perception that a parish is particularly vulnerable to annexation or closure during an interregnum.[1]Throughout the late summer and autumn of 1952, the threat of merger or worse hung heavily over the Annunciation. The church had just come through the war, attendance was still falling, parochial engagement had wound down to an alarming degree. The Sisters of Bethany finally departed in September, at what the P.C.C. minutes for September 25th describe as 'this unfortunate stage of the church's history'.

The war had fortunately brought back an old friend to the Annunciation. For the remainder of the interregnum, the church was left in the capable, but elderly hands of a retired Bishop – Rocksborough Remington Smith (1872-1955), affectionately known as 'Rocky'. His adherence to the Annunciation was not coincidental. Back in the days of the mission, Rocky Smith had grown up there under the guidance of George Chapman, who had directed him towards his priestly vocation. Theologically, throughout his life, he stood firmly alongside his mentor. In the Jubilee Book for the fiftieth anniversary of the church in 1914, he wrote:

> *Father Chapman was consistently loyal to the Church of England, and during those dark days when so many of her sons were leaving for a foreign*

Communion I do not think that his loyalty faltered for a moment. He was convinced that she is a true part of the Catholic Church, and that her priesthood and her Sacraments are undoubtedly valid.

There is no doubt, in his later career, Rocksborough Smith bore the abiding stamp of the Annunciation. One can hear a subliminal memory of its history, regarding the local persecutions which Rocky must have witnessed at first hand in the late nineteenth century, in a sermon he delivered to the Annual Catholic Conference in New York in 1928.

I often think that one reason why the Catholic Revival made such wonderful strides in its early days was because its priests went to the poor and were persecuted. Mobs invaded their churches, egged on by the keepers of beer-houses and owners of houses of vice. Mud and stones were thrown at them. They often had to be protected by the police in the streets. The rulers of the Church, who should have known better, were suspicious of Romish practices, did their best to prevent their teaching and worship, and at best ignored them. The praise of men seldom came their way. Preferment and promotion in the Church was never theirs. Our circumstances are, of course, quite different; and we have to endure none of that on this continent, and I believe we suffer from not having it. A little persecution would do us a world of good, would weed out the half-hearted, would brace us up, would harden us.

After ordination in 1901, Rocksborough Smith had pursued a teaching career as a theologian, and also served for seven years as a parish priest in Dorset. Thereafter, he chose to work in the New World, largely in Canada, where, from 1921, he was Professor of Divinity in Lennoxville. In 1926, he was appointed Bishop of Algoma in Ontario, a post he held until 1940. Approaching retirement, he returned to England during the war, and subsequently decided to remain in Britain as a parish priest in rural Devon. Now, in 1952, at the age of nearly seventy, Rocksborough Smith returned to the Annunciation, the church where he started out as a boy, to support it in its hour of need. During his short stewardship, Rocksborough Smith helped the parish negotiate the anxious months before the recommendations of the Diocesan Organizational Review were made public. The uncertainty must have discouraged any eligible clergy from putting themselves forward for the post, and thus prolonged the interregnum after Father Power's death.

In October, however, Rocky Smith was able to announce the happy news that, in the face of the vehement resistance from the Annunciation and from other local churches under threat, the Diocese had backed down and agreed to modify its plans for re-organisation, but only on the understanding that the stipends for priests in those churches could be maintained. In effect, this meant that the parishes must find the lion's share of those stipends themselves. This, with the rents from the halls, and with its low overheads, the Annunciation has mercifully been able to do ever since.

Bishop Rocksborough Smith, the Annunciation's safe pair of hands in one of its most precarious hours, signed off in January 1953, having led the worship for four months, two more than he had originally intended. He died two years later, in 1955. Father Bullivant wrote a tribute to him in the Parish Magazine:

The Bishop had the greatest love and affection for the Annunciation, where under the saintly Fr. Chapman he learned the Faith, and we are proud of the fact that this parish produced such a wonderful Bishop and champion of the Catholic Faith. His keen interest and love of the Annunciation continued right to the end, and only a few days before his death he had planned to come and preach here on the Sunday following, the Feast of Title. I had much help and encouragement from him during my first year as Vicar and he was delighted to know that our missionary and evangelical teaching followed so closely the pattern laid down by Fr. Chapman.

In his memoir of Father Chapman, written in 1914, Rocky had written about his mentor's relationship with the church:

The congregation of the Annunciation was more like a happy family gathering than I have ever seen elsewhere. All looked up to him as the Father.

For that critical moment in the Annunciation's history, Bishop Rocky was that Father; and who is to say that it was not his presence that held the family together when it was threatened with dispersal? It might seem surprising that the incumbency of the church Rocksborough Smith loved so much was never offered to him. But it was not only a matter of timing. He was a married man, with a family, and that, even in the twentieth century, disqualified him from so Catholic a post in a Wagner church. Nevertheless, the Annunciation afforded him a privilege rarely granted to a priest – a homecoming; and it must have lent his life a sense of completion.

12. FATHER BULLIVANT

THE CHURCHWARDEN who had led the fight against the amalgamation, Victor Bartholomew (sic), wrote in the Parish Magazine for November 1952:

I am sure all of you who were in church on Sunday, October 19th, heard with much rejoicing, and those of you who were not present will be pleased to hear the news that we are to remain a separate parish… Let us now hope and pray that a good and faithful Priest may soon be appointed as our Vicar and take up his duties in the near future. I venture to suggest that never before in our little church's history have things appeared so black, not having a resident Priest or Sisters.

His prayer was swiftly answered. The Bishop of Lewes, Geoffrey Warde, preaching at the Annunciation for Midnight Mass (attended by 76 worshippers, a pleasing number at the time), was able to announce the appointment of a new priest.

The eighth vicar of the Annunciation, Ronald Bullivant, admitted to the *The Brighton Gazette and Herald* in 1984, thirty years into his incumbency, that he had at first been reluctant to become vicar of the parish. 'When I first saw the church my first reaction was to turn it down'. He went home to write to the bishop politely declining the offer, but before he could do so, another letter arrived from Bishop Bell informing him of the day of his installation.

> *Although I felt I wasn't the man for the job, I knew it would be a challenge and decided I had been directed here. God would make up for my inadequacies. And, of course, if you take over a run-down church, you can make more of an impact.*

That impact was enormous. Father Bullivant found himself with a fight on his hands – a church with a reduced congregation and no money, yet expected to pay its own way. When he was first appointed, he asked the then Archdeacon (later Bishop of Lewes) Lloyd Morrell how he should run the parish. Lloyd told him to run it like an Irish Roman Catholic mission. He might well have said 'like the original mission'.

Bullivant was not yet forty when he became vicar in March 1953. He was fortunate in that he took over in the year of Queen Elizabeth II's Coronation. The event enhanced the sense of restoration which had been spreading through Europe in the postwar years. In what was for many their first experience of television, the British people saw the church, the monarchy and their political leaders coming together as one nation. For a brief period, it had a pronounced effect on the numbers going to church, and Father Bullivant, with his prodigious energy, was able to capitalise on this sense of restoration, and to maintain it. In the early years of his incumbency, he started a new social club, revamped the Parish Magazine (now addressing its readers as 'my dear friends', rather than as 'my dear people'), organised days out for the choir and the Confraternity of the Blessed Sacrament, initiated the increasingly popular pilgrimages to the shrine of Our Lady of Walsingham, and enthusiastically engaged with the parish at every level, even following the church football team.[1] His endeavour was rewarded with a steady rise in communicants year on year throughout the Fifties and Sixties, until the numbers were almost back up to Victorian levels. Inspired by Father Bullivant's renewed sense of mission, nuns returned to the Mission House in September 1954, in the shape of five Sisters of the Community of the Holy Name. It was clear that the light had returned to the Annunciation.

Father Bullivant was considered a teaching priest, instructing his congregation not only in doctrinal matters, but in the history of 'the three branches of the Catholic church' and their festivals. His favourite themes: Catholic unity, the race of angels, and latterly, the iniquitous prospect of women's priestly ministry, were repeated in a roughly three-year cycle. But he liked his sermons to be heard in silence. Though he was a sociable priest, who joined in enthusiastically at parish parties, his tolerance of noise in church was very low. The children on whom he vented his spleen were not few in number.

The eighth vicar was a regular champion of the Virgin Mary, whom, he loved to repeat, even Wordsworth described as 'Our tainted nature's solitary boast'. (His newsletters were peppered with the English poets, albeit with a very small stock of quotations). He believed that *The Book of Common Prayer* had excluded the Marian aspect of worship from the Church of England. Anxious to restore it, he often recounted how he had said on his arrival at the Annunciation to the statue of Mary: 'Well, you have got me here, now you must look after the place.' In the early years, he felt that she kept her end of the bargain. So he encouraged the habit that had grown up at the Annunciation of sending birthday cards to Mary. These can still be seen under the statue of Mary on September 8th, her traditional birthday. Father Bullivant once claimed to have met while on holiday in South East Asia an African Bishop who knew the Church of the Annunciation by reputation simply because of this strange Marian habit. The tradition of singing 'Happy Birthday' to the BVM, (as well as to individual members of the congregation) which continues in the church today, may also date from his incumbency.

Father Bullivant was also an unquestioning supporter of Marian visions, leading an annual pilgrimage to Walsingham (where the Blessed Virgin Mary is said to have appeared in a dream to Richeldis in the 11th century), and eagerly preaching on the authenticity and importance of other popular sightings, especially Lourdes, Fatima, La Salette and curiously Garabandal. But this enthusiasm for the miraculous and supernatural could tip over into the ridiculous, when, for example he claimed that a kestrel which had moved into the tower had been divinely sent to solve the church's pigeon problem; or, even more bizarrely, when the Turin Shroud was revealed as a piece of medieval hokum in 1988, claiming that the face of Christ may well have been miraculously printed on the cloth in the Middle Ages as 'a supernatural aid to our faith'.

Liturgically, Father Bullivant continued the Roman rite and the Catholic *Kalendar* at the Annunciation, tolerating none of the compromises that Father Power had entertained. It is said that when a *Book of Common Prayer* was needed for the Bishop for his installation, there wasn't one to be found in the building. This story is probably apocryphal, but it gives us a flavour of the man and his reputation. There was now also regular Benediction, which he celebrated enthusiastically, without interference from the bishop or the neighbourhood. Indeed, Father Bullivant claimed that when Bishop Bell had appointed him to the Annunciation, it was on the understanding that he would continue the Catholic tradition of the parish.[2]

In many ways Father Bullivant ran a parallel Roman church at the Annunciation, as if it were already a full member of the Roman communion, which he considered to be the case, though he knew true Roman Catholics would never have accepted it as such. This did not deter him. 'In our part of the Catholic Church', he was fond of saying, as if he considered the Annunciation, and Anglo-Catholics in general, to be already under papal authority, rather than Canterbury. It was for this reason he thought that the Church of England should be named more correctly 'the Church in England'. When the church orders, we obey', he wrote in 1961, 'To do otherwise would surely be to act as non-conformists.' But he firmly rejected the accusation that the Annunciation was 'extremist', explaining that it depended where the normative lay, and for him it lay with the Vatican.

In 1962, Father Bullivant wrote, in a passage that could serve as his general manifesto:

> *There can be no valid Mass or Holy Communion without a Catholic Priest. A non-conformist Minister may use the same words and perform the same actions, but he is no more capable of consecrating the bread and wine into the Body and Blood of Jesus than is any other layman. It is because we in our portion of the Church have maintained, unbroken, the Catholic Priesthood from the time of the Apostles that we are part of the One True Church and not a new religion created in the time of Henry VIII. At all costs this precious heritage must be defended.*

Bullivant certainly had no truck with the Reformation, nor with the growing interest in inter-faith dialogue. Ecumenism, for Father Bullivant, meant reunification with Rome. He rarely failed to emphasise this in the January Octave, the week set aside for prayers for church unity. In 1961, he withdrew the Annunciation's financial support to the Mission at Accra because he disagreed with the Bishop of Accra's enthusiasm for inviting non-conformist preachers to speak in the cathedral there. In 1964, when a Covenant was proposed between the Anglican Communion and the Methodist Connection, he fought furiously against it, urging the congregation to read the proposals, but also to reject them. It became a obsession for him over several years, dominating his weekly column in the Parish Magazine, until, to his delight, the proposal failed to get the 70% majority it needed in General Synod in 1972. But Bullivant was swimming against the tide. The Covenant was eventually signed in 2003.

In 1963 Father Bullivant went to Rome in Low Week and was granted an audience with Pope John XXIII, (at that time in the midst of the Second Vatican Council) who sent back his special blessing to the Annunciation.

It was recorded in the minutes of the parish AGM for that year:

The work for unity goes ahead and takes many shapes, the Church of England is a true part of the Holy Catholic Church. This is a priceless heritage the truth of which has always been taught and understood at the Annunciation.

Subsequently, as if this were not quite enough, Bullivant scribbled a note beside the minute in his own hand:

and it is of paramount importance that all proposals for unity should have as their ultimate goal, reunion with the Mother Church of Rome. One fold – one shepherd -

The following year Father Bullivant led a parish pilgrimage to Florence, Assisi and Rome, where the Annunciation party was given special seats close to Pope Paul VI's throne (Pope John had died the previous year), and they were specially mentioned among the pilgrims present during the audience. Once again, Father Bullivant, this time with sister Clare, one of the Sisters of the Holy Name, was personally presented to the new pontiff, who through them 'sent greeting and a special blessing to the parish and the community'.

Bullivant welcomed and scrupulously implemented all the recommendations of the Second Vatican Council regarding the liturgy. Though he personally detested change, he was never critical of the Cardinals who ordered it, and, rather like an expatriate, showed a greater allegiance to the authority of the Papal See than many of those already ministering within the Roman fold.

He once cancelled Evensong in Unity Week so that his congregation might go to hear visiting Catholic clergy preach; and in 1986 he invited Father Rea from St Joseph's, the local Catholic church, to celebrate Unity Week with him 'the Annunciation being within the borders of his parish'. The service brought together the congregations of St Joseph's and the Annunciation for the first time. But, when one looks at the order of service now, there can be no doubt that there was no whiff of broader ecumenism in the incensed air.

Father Bullivant's congregation reached a high point in 1963, when over 8000 communions were received, only two thousand short, Father Bullivant was not slow to point out, of Father Fison's record. If sex began in 1963, as Philip Larkin maintained, then perhaps there is a connection here, because from that point on, attendance at the Annunciation and elsewhere in Brighton, began to decline. As the Sixties continued, there was a change too in Father Bullivant's demeanour. The ebullient confidence of his ministry begins to diminish. It is clear where he squarely laid the blame for the declining interest in the church – on the youth culture that had emerged in the late Sixties, and on the parents who seemed unable to control it. In 1974, in his annual report, he wrote:

We are blessed with a most faithful and deeply spiritual group of people who set a very high standard of the Christian ideal and we are only sorry that their noble example is not followed by many of our younger members. It continues to be a source of sadness that so many, within months of confirmation, seem to have forgotten the promises they made to serve God faithfully. However full the church may be, the ones who are expected are frequently noted by their absence, I fear it is a symptom of the materialistic age in which we live. We pray that parents may set a good example and be mindful that all human beings are immortal souls as well as animal bodies. Education is frequently the God to which all else is sacrificed.

It is perhaps difficult now to discern why Father Bullivant targets 'education' at the end of this passage. Did he mean the teaching of science which encourages an empirical, materialist world view? Or is this an oblique swipe at the sex education which was now being offered in the schools?

Father Bullivant's uncompromising beliefs did not sit easily with the young, and the defections he complained of escalated rapidly. A significant factor in the social change Father Bullivant decried was the prescription of the contraceptive pill (which was offered to married women from 1961 and then to single women from 1974). It radically changed sexual and social behaviour amongst the young in Britain and inevitably disinclined the generation that now availed itself of these new freedoms to accept the teaching of the church on these matters, especially the Roman Catholic Church (which Father Bullivant naturally supported). But, further criticism of the eighth vicar's style was to come from a very different, and unexpected source – the Sisters of the Holy Name.

In October 1971, their Reverend Mother Penelope travelled from the mother house in Malvern to meet Father Bullivant. She wished to discuss with him the discontent that was spreading amongst the sisters living in the Mission House in Lincoln Street regarding their work in the parish, and the Marian style of his ministry. Bullivant kept an extensive memorandum of the meeting, in which he notes that the younger sisters were feeling sidelined in terms of parish responsibilities. They had also complained that 'I did not want them to do any instruction etc but wished to do it all myself'. The Reverend Mother had informed him that 'we are a Protestant Community, and older ones only felt at home with our religion. Younger ones found it extreme and particularly emphasis placed on B.V.M. and Benediction'. The old controversy that had dogged the Annunciation under Father Hinde reared its head once more. It is uncanny how deep-seated contradictions can re-emerge in institutions, across generations, as if they were almost a reflex in the building itself.

During the meeting with the Reverend Mother, Father Bullivant pointed out that Benediction was common to all the Wagner churches, and that 'most of the Brighton churches had Benediction (devotions) on Sunday evening'. Uncharacteristically, in what appears to be an attempt to appease the Reverend Mother, Father Bullivant offered her an assurance that the Annunciation was not Roman Catholic[3], and promised that he would not go over to Rome if the proposed union with the Methodists came about. But he also made it clear he would not take part in any service of Reconciliation, noting: 'we should continue to be unreconciled, for which provision was made'.

Father Bullivant spent several weeks brooding on this awkward meeting. When he finally replied to the Reverend Mother[4], he went on the attack, confessing himself perplexed by the remark that 'you are now a Protestant Community', especially given the background of the Holy Name order and 'the aims for which it was founded by Father Herbert'[5]. Bullivant declared himself 'fully aware of all the new "thoughts" of the present day', and of how the basic truths of the Faith were being questioned by members of the Church, but he stood by his immutable Catholic principles:

> But the Faith upon which the Church, this parish and your Community is founded is an unchangeable Faith, and unless we believe and practice the truths of the Catholic faith as enshrined in our official formularies, we surely cannot regard ourselves as loyal members of the Church of England. I have yet to find the word Protestant in our formularies.

At the end of the letter, Father Bullivant expressed the hope that there might be 'at least five members of the Community, not too advanced in years, who would find our teaching not at variance with their beliefs'. But there were not. The writing was on the wall, and less than a year later, in August 1972, Mother Superior Penelope wrote to Father Bullivant regretfully announcing the withdrawal of the sisters, remarking that:

> the small parish of the Annunciation has had sisters in its midst almost continuously for very many years and we feel the praying community that has been built up within your congregation will go faithfully on. In the great new housing areas this work has yet to be accomplished and the needs are tremendous.

Poverty had changed its address. Yet perhaps this was also a plausible excuse for Mother Penelope to extricate her nuns; and the real reasons for the withdrawal were contained in the earlier memorandum and in the response it drew.

The final departure of the sisters in February 1973, after twenty years in the parish, was a bitter blow, from which Father Bullivant felt the Annunciation never fully recovered. Thereafter, the increasing introversion of the church seems to have mirrored his own. In 1977, following a spate of thefts including that of a precious 18th century gilded wooden carving of St Anthony[6] Father Bullivant had brought back from Portugal twenty years previously, the church was locked for the first time. The community no longer had unmediated access to its church, a state of affairs that would have dismayed Father Chapman.

In recognition of his parochial work, however, Ronald Bullivant was made a Canon of Chichester Cathedral in 1978. His ministry seems to have been considerably reinvigorated by the Pope's visit to Britain in 1982. Shortly thereafter, he entered the lists against the rising support for women's priestly ministry in the Church of England, and this would become the dominant theme for the rest of his tenure. 'No sacrament without proper priests', remained his watchword, and that could not include women. Neither could his after-Mass drinks on Christmas Day, when male members of the congregation were annually invited into the Clergy House for sherry with 'F.B.', while the female members were invited to wait for them in the church, or to go home and see to the Christmas dinner. This reveals not only the patriarchal culture that Canon Bullivant sought to maintain, but also how little headway feminism had made at the church up to the late 1980s.

Barry Hewlett-Davies remembers the eighth vicar's annual parties:

He used to have a party every year for everyone where you could have anything you liked to drink – provided it was hot and you could put milk in it. We played games – pass the parcel, a general knowledge quiz and musical chairs to Sir Roger de Coverley. I was excused that on the grounds of arthritis.

But we should not imagine Canon Bullivant only as a stern man, hankering after the values of the Victorian age. Undoubtedly principled, he was not inflexible. A married couple, of whom one partner had been married before, was denied the Sacrament by him for the best part of ten years. Then suddenly, he let them know, not personally, but through his sister, that they would be allowed to communicate.

Canon Bullivant's ministry was hugely supported by two industrious, inter-related families at the church, the Bishops and the Morgans. These extensive clans formed the backbone of the congregation for several decades.[7] Jack Morgan acted stalwartly as churchwarden in the Seventies and Eighties, and saw his eldest son, Martin, mentored by Canon Bullivant, go forward for ordination, one of a long line of priests nurtured at the Annunciation.[8] Jack's younger son, Andrew, eventually served alongside his father as churchwarden, and continued to do so under Bullivant's successor.

Living in the Clergy House with his mother, his sister and her husband, Canon Bullivant led a largely frugal life.[9] Yet he was an ardent traveller. His annual luxury was a long holiday, often in Italy, or the Alps, once to the Holy Land, and latterly in South East Asia, especially Thailand and Bali. He admired the Balinese because of the way they continued to integrate Hinduism into their daily lives, and felt that as Christians, we should do the same with our religion.

The church celebrated the 150th anniversary of the Oxford Movement in 1983, and Canon Bullivant himself wrote a series of articles in the Parish Magazine, explaining the heritage of the Catholic Revival to his contemporary parishioners. The growing disinclination towards the iniquities of the modern world becomes more and more evident in his writing during the fourth decade of his incumbency. As he grew older, Bullivant clearly wrestled with the same demons as Father Hinde about the validity of his Anglican ordination. He was also beginning to feel the stirrings of liberalisation within his own church, speaking with grumpy paranoia in 1985, of 'enemies without and within'. There is some sense too that he was also growing tired of the investment in the outward trappings of Anglo-Catholicism. One parishioner remembered a passage from one of his late sermons:

If you think heaven's going to be like this, you're in for a big surprise... sacraments and services, smells and bells, will cease!

His insistence on the church's loyalty and obedience to Rome became increasingly formulaic and dogmatic towards the end of his life, yet Canon Bullivant still held back from crossing to Rome. Father Ray Blake recalls a conversation in which Canon Bullivant said he very much wanted to be in communion with the Holy See, but:

If I was received into the Catholic Church this evening, I would have to throw into the dustbin that which I had consecrated, honoured as God and knelt before this morning, I just couldn't do that.

It was clear even to Canon Bullivant himself that his ministry was running out of steam. In March 1987 he complained that only ten or twelve worshippers were appearing at Evensong (a service which was to disappear completely from the church after his departure). That summer he was mugged in Sardinia by a thief on a motorcycle and, clinging on to his bag, was dragged along the road for several yards, necessitating his hospitalisation. His sight was also deteriorating. Perhaps he could also sense the impending conflicts over women's ministry which he had first cautioned against as early as 1985, and from the introduction of which he did not think the Church of England would likely survive. Two years later, in 1989, he wrote that he knew it was time for a younger man to take over. He retired to his native Yorkshire, together with his household, with 4000 sermons behind him, aged 76.

Yet, Canon Bullivant could never quite let go of the Annunciation, returning once more in 1994 to celebrate a Golden Jubilee Mass to mark the fiftieth anniversary of his ministry. During his incumbency, Canon Bullivant had fostered several priestly vocations from among the congregation. He saw this as an important part of his ministry. One of these was Carl Davis, who returned to give the sermon at the Jubilee. He described the Canon as the 'epitome of the parish priest'. This might well have served as an epitaph. Ronald Bullivant died the following year in Whitby. The journalist who wrote his obituary in the *Brighton Evening Argus* made an understandable mistake:

A Roman Catholic canon who served in Brighton for 36 years has died.

This would perhaps have delighted the deceased. And it demonstrates that the public at large no longer understood the difference between Anglo and Roman Catholicism. One wonders if they ever really had, perhaps because of priests like Father Bullivant, who saw no difference. Father Cyril Hordern, the assistant priest at the Annunciation for some years under Bullivant, had converted to Roman Catholicism on his deathbed in 1986. But there is no public record that the eighth vicar of the Annunciation followed his example.

13. FATHER DAVID

W E HAVE NOW almost reached our own times, and a writer of history must approach the still undigested years of the recent past with caution, especially because many of the protagonists are still living, and some still in active ministry. The changing demographic of Hanover was one of the greatest problems that faced Canon Bullivant's successor, David Wostenholm, when he took over the parish in 1990. A process of gentrification had been underway in the area since the 1970s. The predilection for mortgages and home ownership brought in many first time buyers in to buy up the small homes that for over a century had been occupied by the poor working classes.

Even though, under his stewardship, the liturgy and ritual at the Annunciation remained resolutely Catholic, Father David, as he liked to be known (breaking with tradition[1]), did not exclude those of other faiths. He had come from the multicultural parish of Leytonstone to the Annunciation, and, more in the spirit of the times, he was not in the least opposed to inter-faith dialogue. He was quick, for example, to support the Churches Together in England initiative when it was set up in 1990. In 1993 he welcomed a prominent ecumenist from the Roman Catholic tradition, the Catholic Bishop of Arundel (the future Archbishop of Westminster and thereby Catholic Primate of England),

Cormac Murphy-O'Connor, to preach at the Annunciation in Unity Week. But Father David's view on reunification with Rome seems to have been very different from that of his predecessor. In a guide he provided for the visitors from St Joseph's, the local Roman Catholic church, he wrote:

We are separated from you by history and discipline, but we are inseparably WITH you 'in communion of mind and heart' in the building up of the Lord's Kingdom.

David's ecumenism went much deeper than his predecessor's, and he came to welcome other denominations. He encouraged the lay-preaching of Simon Barrow, co-director of Ekklesia, the progressive Christian think tank. Simon's wife, Carla Roth, came from a Mennonite background, and was a prominent member of the P.C.C. Father David even invited people from other faith groups to use the church as a sacred space, which drew at least one local Taoist, Jane Launchbury, into the congregation and into the Mass. Jane was an energetic member of the Hanover community and editor of the local community newspaper, *The Hanover Herald*. She became a key link for Father David.[2] With her help, slowly but surely, he began to harness the energy of the by now largely secular community around him. Most tellingly, he re-established strong links with the local community centre (the original Annunciation Boys School on Southover Street). He also engaged with the local council, and put the church at the heart of Hanover Day. This was an annual celebration David co-founded for the area, a street party that encompassed Coleman Street, Washington Street and Southover Street[3]. He even allowed the Morris Men to enter the church at the end of Mass to begin the street procession that opened the festival on Hanover Day. This began with a lap of the nave, during which the statue of the Blessed Virgin was hoisted onto the shoulders of four of the congregation to be paraded through the streets in the company of a local samba band. The feeling was that of a religious procession that you might see in Assisi or Rio. (Father David had visited Brazil in the late 1990s and had interested himself in the liberation theology of the favelas.)

In the early years at the Annunciation, Father David's tenure was rocked by the divisive issue of the ordination of women into the Church of England. This was particularly problematic for the Catholic tradition within the Anglican communion. Attitudes to gender and sexuality had changed dramatically in society during Father Bullivant's time, especially rapidly in a city like Brighton, and the Annunciation's former priest had done nothing to engage with those changes. But, inevitably, these new social values were strongly represented in Father David's congregation, and he was at least prepared to listen to them. In July 1993, he took the unprecedented step, which his predecessor would never have contemplated, of allowing a parishioner, Helen Nevitt, to put the case for women's ordination in the Parish Magazine, albeit with his own closely reasoned counter arguments appending it.

The first women were ordained in the Church of England in 1994. Invoking the spirit of Father Chapman, Wostenholm wrote in the Parish Priest's annual report that year:

> *While I am pastor here, I will welcome discussion, difference of opinion and even argument on this matter, but not division. I will not tolerate the setting up of opposing camps on this issue, and I do not intend to let this single issue cripple the mission of the Church, as long as I feel it has a mission.*

The congregation heeded his words, and the tone was set for the rest of his incumbency. The differences were tolerated, but only because those in favour of women's priestly ministry did not push to overturn the resolutions the church had signed up to preventing the ministry of women at the Annunciation. The issue did not split the Annunciation communion. Instead, there was greater community involvement, pilgrimages to Assisi and to Rouen and Chartres, and even, on one memorable occasion in 1998, a glitter party in the Clergy House to celebrate Father David's birthday. The Hanover Days were particularly satisfying, with the church open all day once more to its community. For one afternoon a year, it became the thoroughfare from Washington Street to Coleman Street, and live entertainment was provided in the north aisle, which had been cleared of pews in a reordering designed to create a flexible space for concerts and exhibitions.

As Father David's links with the community strengthened, the parish around him was becoming increasingly affluent and gentrified. He found himself in the historically ironic position of having to call for affordable local housing for poorer families in a community that had specially been created for them by Father Wagner. In a letter to *The Argus* in 1996 he wrote about the local Phoenix Brewery site which was earmarked for social housing, but on the condition a third of it would be designated for office development:

> *There are many other community groups who have need of this sort of accommodation which is increasingly difficult to find. In an age of 'stay at home' individualism, such groups should be positively encouraged. I would also like to outline another need, particular in this area of dense population and steep hills – the provision of sheltered accommodation for the frail*

elderly who would like to stay around the close knit community they have known most of their lives.

This gives us another snapshot of the area of Hanover, and the enormous demographic changes that were taking place at the end of the twentieth century. By the turn of the millennium, only twenty per cent of the congregation attending the Annunciation lived in Hanover, whereas it had been near 100 per cent in the 1860s. Today that percentage is even smaller.

It must be said that Father David's energies never flagged in defending traditional parish life. He loved the Annunciation and the church loved him. Regardless of the dramatic changes taking place in the demography of the parish, it was a time of great harmony for the Annunciation 'family', and perhaps even for wider Hanover. But, during the boom years of the late 1990s, as the area became more and more beholden to the property market, Father David must have realised he was fighting a losing battle. The old Hanover families were cashing in on the boom and moving away. In 2002, at the Bishop's bidding, David left the Annunciation to take over All Saints Hove, the central church in Hove. It was not a felicitous move. Father David found himself uncomfortable ministering to 'the carriage folk' of Hove, who had a much looser Anglo-Catholic tradition (and even an early Sunday service based on *The Book of Common Prayer*). His heart remained at the Annunciation. In a letter to *The Evening Argus* the year after he left the parish, he wrote pungently:

When I lived in the area (Hanover), I supported a local project to fight graffiti and I must confess to being tempted to add some comments on the hoarding outside the Technical College building advertising more luxury homes when local people can no longer afford to buy in the area. I will, of course, resist this temptation.

David was a latter-day apostle of the Oxford Movement, and a member of the Society of the Holy Cross, the organization, formed in 1855, that became the driving force behind the movement. He combined his Catholicism with a radical energy that the movement had intellectually aspired to, but rarely attained, even in the nineteenth century, an energy not seen at the Annunciation since George Chapman, whom he greatly admired. When David subsequently returned to his native Scotland to lead a parish in a downtrodden area of Glasgow, it was as if the spirit of Father Chapman were calling him back to his proper vocation.

After David Wostenholm there were three interregna at the Annunciation in rather quick succession. The pastoral continuity in the first two decades of the twenty-first century has been provided by the assistant priest, Richard Clarke (ably supported in his endeavours by his wife Diana). Father Richard's lucid sermons continue to deserve a wider audience.

As the pre-war generation died away, there seemed to be little enthusiasm for the Annunciation's brand of ritualistic religion among the baby boomers. The last full-time vicar of the church was the affable Father David Hawthorn, who stayed for less than two years, from 2002-4, finding the South unconducive. He also regretted the lack of schools in the parish (ironic given that, in the nineteenth century the Annunciation had itself once housed schools with two to three hundred pupils), and wondered why so few people greeted him in the street.

Despite the fact that the parish could now pay a full contribution for its clergy, the living was suspended by the Diocese in 2007 and a licensed priest-in-charge was appointed. The link with the community became more tenuous again after David Wostenholm's departure. This was not entirely due to the lack of coherent leadership in the church's ministry in the new century, but also to the fact that further demographic changes were taking place in Hanover. As the recession began to bite, the radical young middle-class couples, who had been such willing partners in David Wostenholm's community actions, began to disappear. There were more buy-to-lets, more rented multiple occupancies, and a massive influx of transient students. Hanover Day, which David had instigated, was no longer an annual event, and at the time of writing, seems to have disappeared completely. It was not the church, but the community itself that had begun to wither, with the result that the church in recent years has become rather isolated in a city that in 2012 was dubbed by its local newspaper the most godless in Britain.

The sanctuary before Father Tiley's re-ordering

The sanctuary after the addition of the reredos. Note the truncation of the Burne-Jones window

The Rood – Christ on the Vine
Father Tiley's addition in the 1920s

Father Fison's 1895
memorial notice
showing Christ crucified
on the wine press

86

Edwin Power
Seventh Vicar

Church of the Annunciation of Our Lady
WASHINGTON STREET, BRIGHTON.

—::—

Day of Offering:
THURSDAY, 20th August, 1942.

—::—

AN APPEAL!

THE Parish Priest will sit in Church all day from 7.30 a.m. until 8 p.m. to receive gifts. Will you please give as liberally as you can to enable us to carry on the work of the Church in these difficult days. Our needs are great, so please do your best. If you are unable to bring your offering, please send it to the Rev. Edwin A. Power, The Annunciation Vicarage, Washington Street, Brighton 7.

EDWIN A. POWER,
Vicar.

John E. Strong,
W. C. Harper,
Churchwardens.

Wartime Day of Offering Notice

VE Day Street Party, Hanover

Bishop Remington Rocksborough Smith, 'Rocky',
and William Temple, Archbishop of York, and later of Canterbury

Open air Benediction at Walsingham. Father Bullivant, kneeling, centre right

Father Ronald Bullivant Eighth Vicar
with Sister Clare of The Community of the Holy Name meeting Pope Paul VI 1964

Canon Bullivant with the B.V.M. in the church 1984

Father David Wostenholm Ninth Vicar 1998

Hanover Day Procession

Members of the choir in full voice in 2008

Some of the present congregation on a day-trip to Portsmouth

Father Michael 'Spike' Wells and Bishop Martin Warner

Spike with Marcia Bellamy Artistic Director of the Annunciation Festival 2014

14. THE NEW MILLENNIUM

ALARGE PICTURE dominates the east wall of the north aisle of the Annunciation. It is a copy of *The Adoration of the Shepherds*, by Gherardo della Notte (a.k.a. Gerrit Van Honthorst) painted during the Counter-Reformation in the seventeenth century. The official copy was made in the Uffizi in 1911/12 by Anselmo Guerrieri. It may have been purchased by a visitor from the Annunciation to Florence just before the First World War. It has hung undisturbed on the wall ever since, and its surface is covered with the black deposit of over a century of candle-smoke, dust and incense. As I write, it is being cleaned, revealing the intense chiaroscuro of the original. Cherubim circle above the shepherds receiving the upward reflected light from the Christ child. It is not difficult to see why this image was chosen by its donor for the church – it reflects the centrality of the Incarnation, a key Oxford Movement theme.

In many ways, the copied painting stands as a metaphor for the overall intention of the church. Reviewing the Annunciation's historical trajectory, and that of the Oxford Movement from which it sprung, one might imagine that one is observing the certainties of faith of the nineteenth century gradually coming into conflict with the scientific gaze of the twentieth and the cultural relativism of the twenty-first. But, in fact, what we may be looking at is actually something much older – the last gasp of the Counter-Reformation, that is, an attempt to reach back to the fixed, god-centred cosmos of the Middle Ages. In much the same way the pre-Raphaelite movement, tried to return to a style of painting developed before the Renaissance[1], the Catholic Revival in England was looking back at least to the days of King Charles the Martyr, if not beyond them, to before Henry VIII and the Dissolution of the Monasteries, in an attempt to re-establish the certainty of the priest-entrusted faith which the Reformation had disrupted.

The religion of the Annunciation, and of the Anglo-Catholic movement itself, provides a copy of an older version of belief reaching back to the 'faith of our fathers'. Father Bullivant's notion that a miracle had imprinted the face of Christ on the Turin Shroud in the Middle Ages serves as a kind of model of thought for the regressive reflex of the Catholic Revival in general – nineteenth century belief projecting itself back onto late medieval belief, which had itself falsified evidence of the life of Christ and the crucifixion.

But, as we have seen in this account, this regressive cultural intention is not necessarily the same as the intention to return the Church of England to Rome. In observing the relations between Arthur Wagner's project and the official Church of England, in which the Annunciation, given its size, played a surprisingly significant role, we can observe a shifting dynamic, sometimes towards, sometimes away from Rome. The argument in the church has always been about the nature of its Catholicism. Was its real intention to rediscover an older, profoundly English Catholicism or to return to Rome?

During the research for this history the present writer has found some evidence that there were a minority involved in the Wagner project, including clergy at the Annunciation, whose intention it was to translate their congregations to Rome. But this investigation has also shown there were many more who did not, who saw their Catholicism as being distinct, and who believed with Richard Hooker, the Anglican divine, that the communion of the Church of England was a gift from God. With the exception of Father Hinde, who we must assume came to the church with the best of intentions, and perhaps Father Bullivant, who was increasingly her proxy advocate, there were very few other clergy who longed to be the agents of the Vatican. Many wore the biretta (Brighton priest John Purchas, we must remember, was convicted just for carrying one in 1870), and most must have flirted with the idea of 'poping' in their darkest moments, but the overwhelming majority stayed, with Arthur Wagner, in the Anglo-Catholic fold. Cynics might argue they did this out of expediency to protect their livings and their pensions. But this account has shown a great deal of faith, and very little expediency among the priests of the Annunciation. In addition, it is patently also not the case that the church merely operated as a Trojan Horse for Catholicism in the community of Hanover. On the contrary, we have seen that it played the biggest role in creating that community, and has continued to do so right down to Father Wostenholm's time with the founding of Hanover Day.

George Chapman, the spiritual father of the Annunciation and the mentor of so many of its priests, certainly saw his faith as being lodged in the Church of England. R.S. his biographer, writes:

The secession... of one of the clergy of the Annunciation to the Roman communion[2], *was a most terrible grief to the vicar; personally attached as he was to the seceder, he grieved for him as well as the parish. Himself so loyal and so true to the English Church, he was always sorely hurt when anyone proved false to her.*

I think this would also have been William Carey's reaction, loyal to the Catholic faith and the Sacrament, respectful of, but not beholden to Rome. It demonstrates a distinct Anglo-Catholic sensibility which has always found its home at the Annunciation. The Roman Catholic view of that sensibility is not always charitable. This may be discerned from an letter (the date has no year) Father Bullivant received from the Roman convert Herbert Hamilton Maughan[3], Provost of the Catholic Social Group, a now defunct intellectual pressure group within Roman Catholicism. Rather wickedly perhaps, the letter has been left in the Annunciation archives for future generations to ponder:

I am so glad to hear that you are still keeping the Papalist banner floating steadily in Brighton. It is sad that Brighton – once a Catholic stronghold, – is now merely a hive of High Church Anglicanism. I think we owe this sad change to George Bell – of evil memory. Tiley was a good influence while he lasted...

I quote this malevolent attack on a highly principled and courageous bishop[4] here not only to illustrate the vituperation which surrounded the Brighton churches well into the last century, but also to highlight the different perceptions of 'Catholicism' that have moved through our church. Once again the shibboleth of High Church is lazily invoked to a tradition of ritualistic observance of which the writer does not approve. Father Bullivant's waspish correspondent is acknowledging here that the translation of congregations like that of the Annunciation to Rome has foundered. But this does not mean, for the present author at least, that the Catholic Revival within the Church of England was by any means a failure. One need only look round today at those many churches in the Diocese and beyond, including the Anglican Cathedrals, where the Blessed Sacrament is reserved, Benediction practised, where portable lights are carried and incense swung, to know that the revival, which Father Wagner promoted so assiduously, has hugely enriched the Anglican Communion.

The bells of the Annunciation fell silent in September 1956, having been deemed unsafe for further pealing. They have never been repaired. There is something symbolic in this, as if the Victorian confidence in religious life was finally exhausted. The two World Wars, and the iniquities that had attended them, had made faith unfashionable. The brief impetus towards spiritual renewal in Britain after the Coronation petered out, as the needs of even the poorest families, which churches like the Annunciation had once tended to, were now catered for by the Welfare State. Macmillan's speech 'You've never had it so good' in 1957 set the seal on a profoundly materialist age.

The new prosperity rendered the Annunciation's mission to the poor virtually redundant. The liberalisation of sexual morality ushered in with the Sixties, the emancipation of women, which gathered momentum in the Seventies and Eighties, the extension of gay rights, the cultural mobility fostered by the global market, all these huge social changes have made the patriarchal teachings of the Western Church unpalatable, and left its leaders floundering, unsure how much ground to concede to popular opinion. This confusion has been compounded in the Diocese of Chichester by the discovery of the clerical abuse of children and juveniles, and by accusations of systemic cover-up. For many, the Church has forfeited its moral authority. In consequence, the Annunciation stands marooned in the neighbourhood it once helped create, with many of those who live around it never even having been inside the building.

At a time when the Church of England is recasting its attitudes towards women's episcopacy, softening its line towards gay marriage (when even the Roman Catholic Church itself, under Pope Francis, is beginning to respond to ideas of social diversity and inclusion), the Anglo-Catholic movement will find itself in a curiously anachronistic position if it does not follow this spirit of change. Where will its next generation of worshippers come from, we might ask, if it continues to defend the socially indefensible in the name of faith?

Yet the remaining Wagner churches in Brighton have now circled their wagons, preparing to defend 'the faith of our fathers' against the social compromises they perceive being made in other parts of the Anglican communion.[5] In 2010, in the presence of Bishop Linday Urwin, the Wagner churches co-signed a covenant reasserting their commitment to the faith handed down through the Apostolic Succession. The Annunciation did not sign this covenant, but remains an associate of the Wagner group. The little church that has historically punched above its weight is still deeply grounded in its Catholic faith, but it hovers on the brink of change.

After a recent animated discussion over women's episcopacy, a deacon, trained at the Annunciation, observed to me wistfully, 'There's no longer a place for liberal Catholics in our tradition'. I hope this is not true. But we must ask: can an Anglo-Catholic church reform itself quickly enough to embrace a society that insists on gender and sexual equality? Can it even remain inside an increasingly liberalising Church of England? Arthur Wagner's first mission in Bread Street, we may recall, was dedicated to Mary Magdalene. Is it conceivable that the Marian tradition at a church like the Annunciation could broaden itself to include Mary Magdalene's discipleship? These are all questions for the future.

Through the streets of Hanover, the Angelus bell rings out regularly as a conscious reminder of what had been the hub of a residential community where regular worship was once the rule, not the exception. The Annunciation mission began surrounded by sectarian suspicion. Now there is a different challenge, by no means unique to Hanover – secular indifference. In an age where the young are drawn, if they are drawn at all, to the evangelical end of the Anglican spectrum, the outlook for ritualistic Anglo-Catholicism looks bleak. But this little church has been through difficult times before; and there is something unique in its prayerful atmosphere which successive bishops have been reluctant to lose.

Arthur Wagner's whitewashed mission has now survived for a century and a half. It has brought comfort and inspiration to so many, and its faith has spread abroad. The mustard seed has indeed become the tree Father Wagner hoped for, where souls, both of the dead and of the living, have found rest. I hope that this account has shown that the Church of the Annunciation is unique and worthy of preservation, both as a historical monument, as the most perfect example of a church planted by the Oxford Movement, but also as a holy place that holds the spirit like no other in Brighton. Those, like myself, who worship there still feel the Real Presence, not only in the Mass, but at unexpected moments, as likely on the stairs to Father Chapman's Memorial Room as on the High Altar where the Sacrament is now reserved. May it continue to be a place where this presence is felt for many generations to come. This 150th year will hopefully mark not only an anniversary but also a new chapter in the relationship between the Annunciation and the people of Brighton and Hove.

APPENDIX 1

THE MUSIC OF THE ANNUNCIATION

F ROM ITS very beginning the Annunciation has had a strong musical tradition. One of the rafters in an early photograph of the interior of the church carries the inscription:

He set singers before the Altar that they might make sweet Melody and daily sing Praises in their Songs

I suspect the hand of Christopher Thompson, the musical first curate of the Annunciation, in the choice of this verse from Ecclesiasticus (47:9).[1] It doesn't sound like one Father Chapman's favourites. The fortunes of the church's music broadly reflect the character of the priests who commission it. It comes and goes, welcomed, then repressed, then encouraged again, depending on whether the incumbent saw it as an enhancement to the liturgy, or suspected it as a distraction from the congregation's proper focus on the Sacrament.

In the same way the Annunciation provided bright colourful ritual for its earliest congregation as a diversion from the grimness of their environment, the music of the Annunciation began at a high level too. Christopher Thompson started his curacy by introducing regular Gregorian chant into the services. It was a field in which he was already something of an expert. It must have had a powerful effect on the fledgling congregation, many of whom would never before have heard chant or experienced its hypnotic effect.

The success of the choir (which numbered 38 singers by the end of 1865, the Annunciation's first year in operation), is evident from the fact that at the grand opening of St Bartholomew's, nearly a decade later, it was Thompson who organised the music for the event. It was 'rendered by a special choir of 120 voices, selected from the choirs attending the different High Churches in the town'. The backbone of this choir was provided by singers from Thompson's own regular choir at the Annunciation. Ironically, by promoting their new sister church, the Annunciation singers were probably encouraging the depopulation of their own. Father Thompson was to leave the following year, in 1875, and the church itself was about to enter the doldrums, both liturgically and musically.

Father Chapman came to the church's spiritual rescue, but it cannot be said that his stewardship greatly advanced the musical culture of the Annunciation. In keeping with his prayerful and unostentatious style of worship, he dispensed with what he saw as the overcomplicated church music of his predecessor. He cultivated prayerful silence, and, in his 'mission services', favoured lusty congregational hymn-singing over chant or polyphony. But the choir was still necessary to bolster the singing in the pews. Chapman saw it as a cohesive force in the community. He presented each member with a gift on their birthdays.[2] The choirboys were given an annual 'treat', an outing to a local beauty spot as a reward for their endeavours.[3] Father Chapman also established an organ fund. There are some accounts of musical entertainments among the parishioners during his incumbency, over which kept a close eye. He strongly disapproved of dancing, and fulminated at anyone who ventured a saucy song at a parish entertainment.

It was not until the arrival of Father Chapman's successor, Father Fison, in 1891, that the wider musical life of the Annunciation began to flourish again. Fison oversaw the formation of the Annunciation Minstrels, formed mainly from members of the choir who provided more secular entertainment at the 'Treats' and parish festivals. The Minstrels seem to have made themselves scarce during the austere incumbency of Henry Hinde.[4]

During the aftermath of the clerical desertion, Father Carey was able to build the choir back to near its original Victorian numbers, but, as we have seen, the war thwarted its development. Carey was no slouch as a singer himself, as Rev. Basil Shelley, his assistant, reports in 1914:

We used to have the Gregorian Plainsong chants and the officiating priest had to intone them. I found this task too complicated and on more than one

occasion I was grateful to my Vicar who was musical and had a good voice,
who came to my assistance and relieved me of the burden.

This testimony also tells us that the tradition of plainsong, started fifty years before at the Annunciation by Christopher Thompson, had not disappeared by this time.

The choir recovered swiftly as the men returned from the Great War. To hear their voices in the services of thanksgiving must have been a heartening sound. But it was on Father Tiley's watch in the 1920s that the major change in the musical culture of the Annunciation took place. In re-ordering the sanctuary, Tiley chose to remove the choir-stalls. The choir was displaced into the organ chapel, where it sang (from two rows of pews facing each other) separated by screens, both from the congregation and from the business of the altar. This was not an attempt to sideline the choir. To Tiley's ear, it provided a more ethereal, transcendental sound in keeping with the atmosphere of the bestowing of the Sacraments. He encouraged the choir greatly in their new chantry, even bringing in an orchestra for some high days and holidays. So keen on the quality of the liturgical music was Father Tiley that he secured the purchase of a new organ. Father David Wostenholm writes about this, in his notes to the artefacts of the church drawn up in 1996:

As can be seen from the specification, the organ was not designed for any more than congregational accompaniment and it would seem that Father Tiley was continuing along the lines of his predecessors with a simple form of music appropriate to the Mission nature of this Church, in contrast to some of the other Anglo-Catholic Brighton churches.

One need only look back to Christopher Thompson and to William Carey to call this into question; and, given Tiley's penchant for the baroque, with his use of orchestra in the Mass, it may also be a misreading of the fifth vicar's intentions. The Annunciation's organ may not be the grandest of instruments, but within its modest acoustic, when properly maintained, it is capable of great sweetness and clarity, and is entirely suited to intricate choral work as well as congregational singing. When an electric organ was tested in the church in 2008, the regular organists John Ross and Nick Houghton both decided in favour of the warm resonance of the existing instrument. The electric model was returned to the manufacturer, and Tiley's organ, made by Morgan and Smith, was duly refurbished.

In the 1940s, under Father Power, like so much else in the parish, the musical tradition of the Annunciation seems to have waned again. The vicar was often to be found in the Parish Magazine, making regular, but presumably fruitless, appeals for men and women to join the choir. The electric blower for the organ was also proving temperamental. The exigencies of the war may also supply part of the reason for the decline in the Annunciation's music. In the Parish Magazine for June 1942, we find the following item:

> *The appointment of Miss van Heedeghem announced in last month's magazine has come to an end. She writes 'Since accepting the post of Organist and Choir Mistress at the Church of the Annunciation of our Lady, I have had to take up work of National importance and thus find I have not sufficient time in which to train the Choir to the musical standard which is required and hereby tender my resignation.'*

It may be disingenuous to wonder whether Miss van Heedeghem's work of National importance was real, or whether it was merely a convenient excuse for extricating herself, after less than a month, from the desultory state in which she found the organ and the choir. Father Power was forced to rely, and not for the first time, on Mr W.C. Harper, churchwarden, organist, stalwart of the choir and veteran of WWI (he had been gassed on the Western Front) who had been holding the fort before she arrived.

The Annunciation had to wait for nearly another decade for the next real flowering of its music. It began with Power's appointment of the organist Norman King. The eldest member of the present choir, Bill Verrier, now in his nineties, joined Norman's choir in 1951, and still speaks highly of his choral organization and musicianship. Perhaps further inspired by the Coronation, and by the social cohesion of the Fifties, the robed choir increased and prospered under King. Father Bullivant paid tribute to him and to the choir when Norman King stepped down at Easter 1958, speaking of 'the wonderful way in which our choir make such a worthy contribution to the worship of the Church'.

Church music at the Annunciation seems to have maintained a good level into the next decade. The Parish Magazine for January 1959 reports:

> *The Choir-boys sang a new Mass for the first time on the Feast of the Immaculate Conception. The Mass was composed by our Organist Mr Chatfield, and lots of people have expressed their delight and appreciation.*

Alas, there is no longer a copy of this Mass setting at the church. Mr G. Chatfield was perhaps the last organist to be held in high regard by Father Bullivant. But he stayed for only three years, departing in 1961. With the advent of rock 'n' roll in Britain, church singing soon became unfashionable among the young, and by the mid-Sixties halcyon days of youth culture, the boys choir appears to have atrophied completely. Thereafter, on high days, singing was occasionally undertaken by an invited boys choir from St John's School.

Even in high periods, a church choir can be perceived as becoming too powerful within a parish church, and many priests are nervous of the shift of focus away from the liturgy it can occasion. It was perhaps for this reason, in the 1990s, after Father Bullivant's departure, that Father David Wostenholm did not encourage the reformation of an established choir. Instead, much in the vein of his mentor Father Chapman, he greatly encouraged the congregational singing he felt the organ suited, sometimes stopping the hymn in the first verse with the admonition 'Start again!', when he felt the congregation weren't pulling their weight. Throughout Father David's tenure, a scratch adult choir led the singing, standing just outside the organ chapel, as if asking permission to rejoin the congregation. Occasionally there would be solo contributions from gifted instrumentalists and soloists to augment the worship. It was not unknown for David himself to sing at the annual Christmas dinner and cabaret in the church hall, most notably, one year – a moving version of Noël Coward's *London Pride*, while somewhat incongruously dressed in his native kilt.

These ad hoc musical arrangements continued until the arrival of Father Steven Foster in 2005. Foster, an accomplished church musician and published composer of church music himself, appointed the opera singer and choral conductor Marcia Bellamy as Director of Music in 2007. Under their joint aegis, the choir began to grow again. In 2009 it moved to its present position by the War Altar in order to re-engage with the congregation after over eighty years in the chantry. Father David Wostenholm, returning to the church to give the homily at the funeral of former churchwarden Fred Sayers,[5] pointed in the direction of the current choir stalls and declared: 'I would never have allowed that!' Marcia has subsequently re-introduced occasional plainchant to the choir. Surely Christopher Thompson must posthumously approve.

Father Steven did much to encourage Marcia and to restore the musical tradition at the Annunciation which continues to thrive under Father Michael Wells, a.k.a Spike Wells, the renowned jazz-drummer, a frequent performer at Ronnie Scott's and former member of the Tubby Hayes Quartet.

The Annunciation Choir now sings Eucharist every Sunday and annually visits Chichester Cathedral in October to sing Evensong. This relationship will shortly become reciprocal. In 2012, Marcia's and the present author's son, Raphael, became a Chichester Cathedral Chorister, the first representative of the Annunciation ever to do so. He will return with the Cathedral Choir in January 2015 to sing Evensong as part of the church's 150th anniversary celebrations.

APPENDIX 2

THE ART OF THE ANNUNCIATION

PARISH CHURCHES build up a collection of artefacts over time, often gifted in memory of faithful parishioners at the time of their death, inherited from other churches that have been closed, or brought back from pilgrimages. The Annunciation is no different in this regard, but what is remarkable about its collection, at least up until WWII, is its aesthetic consistency. Until the turn of the century, the church was in the gift of Father Arthur Wagner, and so it is not surprising the artistic embellishment of the church should reflect his taste, and that of the Catholic Revival he championed. But even after his death in 1902, there seem to be certain leitmotifs that dominate the additions at the Annunciation, and to some extent, in the Wagner churches in general. While researching the artwork of the church, I discovered, for example, that both St Barts and the Annunciation possess reproductions of Della Notte's *The Adoration of the Shepherds*, and Murillo's *Madonna and Child*. These were purchased after Arthur Wagner's death, and after Father Hinde's departure. There are a few key images that seem to have been irresistible to the followers of the revival, and these appear repeatedly in their churches. That is not to say that they somehow contain an encrypted message in the manner of the Da Vinci code. But they do carry a particular intention – to emphasise the Incarnation. They are primarily intended to encourage adoration, to further enhance the reception of 'the Real Presence'. They are also, largely, images drawn either from the Counter-Reformation, or from the pre-Raphaelites, that is, both artistic movements that looked back to the Middle Ages, when the old Catholic religion was still intact.

The Windows

The pride of place at the church has always been taken by the Burne-Jones stained glass window above the High Altar. This takes the Annunciation as its theme. The design is unmistakably pre-Raphaelite. The triple lancet window was put in place in 1865 in memory of one of the mission's first communicants. The inscription reads:

In memory of Elizabeth Austin Attree died 3rd November 1865

Elizabeth Attree was the wife of Thomas Attree, who lived in the Attree Villa at the top of Queen's Park and whose family owned much of the land in the area.

According to Morris and Co's catalogue of designs, now in a private collection in California, the whole of the window was designed by Burne-Jones and executed by Morris, Marshall, Faulkner & Co (an earlier manifestation of the William Morris and Company to which the execution of the window is usually attributed). Burne-Jones and Rossetti were partners in the original company, which may account for the fact that, for many years, it was claimed that Dante Gabriel Rossetti had designed the central light, and the flanking lights only by Burne-Jones. This was based on the clear assertion by Charlotte St John in her account, *Earliest Days* in 1914:

The window was by Morris, the centre light being designed by Dante Gabriel Rossetti, an old schoolfellow of Mr Anderson's.

This is Father Charles Anderson, one of the first curates at the Annunciation. Do we believe (the usually reliable) Miss St John's version or the information lodged in the Morris and Co catalogue? I tend to favour Miss St John's account, simply because she had been around at the time of the window's installation, and took the trouble to elaborate on the local connection when she remembered it in 1914. It is noteworthy that the angels depicted in the left light are playing portative organs, complete with bellows, instruments popular in the Middle Ages, and therefore of interest to the Pre-Raphaelites.

The Morris & Co catalogue also tells us that the windows were renovated in 1888. In Father Tiley's time the Burne-Jones windows were incorporated in the present golden reredos on the High Altar. But something seems to have gone awry in the execution. The central light was lowered to fit inside the reredos, thus compromising the windows' beautiful proportions (for a comparison, see the photographs of the sanctuary on page 85). This also meant that the dedication to Elizabeth Attree had to be squashed into the two side lights. Two cobalt panels then had to be affixed on the original glass at the bottom of these two lights to compensate for the lowering. The overall effect is squat, truncated, and rather bodged. It it hard to know if all this was done by accident or design, but somewhere behind all the gilded wood, the original lights are still in place, awaiting their liberator.

Dating from 1883, the stained glass windows above the altar in the Holy Name Chapel depict 1) The Adoration of the Lamb 2) The Crucifixion 3) The Mass, reinforcing the Oxford Movement's insistence on Christ's real presence in the Mass and the adoration that is appropriate for it. Above these is a roundel showing the Madonna and Child with a suggestion of the Nativity. The windows are unattributed. I have already discussed the significance of this window in chapter 4 above.

Immediately below the Oxford Movement windows, and appended to them by the 'and also' of its inscription is a contemporaneous brass memorial to Cecil Wray of St Martin-in-the-Fields Liverpool. Chapman had spent his first curacy at St James the Less, its daughter church. Wray, a great pioneer of the Catholic Revival in the city, had been his first priestly mentor. As his correspondence shows, Chapman never lost his affection for St James the Less and its congregation, and, despite his spiritual father status at the Annunciation, perhaps always hankered to return to this congregation and to his native Liverpool. In the 1880s, however, when he was offered its incumbency, he turned it down, preferring to stay at the Annunciation.

Throughout the church, we find four further collections of stained glass. The most accomplished of these, on the north, south and east walls of the church, are the twelve apostles, a commission that must have been given during the Renovation of 1881-3. Again the significance is apparent for the Catholic Revival and the Oxford Movement, which insisted on the Apostolic Succession. The twelfth apostle was Judas Iscariot, who of course is missing, and has been replaced here by St James the Less (in Catholic tradition the son of Mary Cleopas, one of the women at the foot of the Cross). The window is inscribed as a memorial to the Reverend H.S. Bramah, Chapman's vicar (after Cecil Wray) at St James the Less in Liverpool. The other windows in the apostle sequence are inscribed in memoriam of members of the church's early congregation (i.e. her own 'apostles'), including R. St John, one of Charlotte St John's family. Attempts have been made to attribute these windows to

Charles Eamer Kempe, whose workshop was very active at the time. However, they do not have his trademark wheatsheaf motif. Kempe's records were disposed of in 1934 when the firm he founded closed in 1934, so we cannot verify this one way or the other.

We know for certain that the large east window, depicting Christ calling the disciples from amongst the fishermen, was transposed from St Nicholas Brighton in 1882. The inscription on a brass plaque below reads:

> *This window originally erected in the ancient parish church of Brighton, the Revd. H.M. Wagner being then vicar, was presented to the Church of the Annunciation by the vicar and churchwardens –*

The window, originally installed by Richard Cromwell Carpenter at St Nicholas' in 1854, was removed to the Annunciation in 1882, during the renovation. At that time, a new sequence of stained glass was being installed at St Nicholas, designed by Charles Eamer Kempe. (These installations took place between 1878-1887). It is doubtful that an artist of Kempe's reputation would have accepted the interpolation of the Carpenter window (or the relocation of the St Joseph and St John the Baptist windows, *see below*) into a sequence of apostles. The Annunciation, relatively poor church that she still was, seems to have been the recipient of the cast-offs from other churches. During the expansion, as far as stained glass was concerned, the policy seems to have been: the more the merrier, rather than trying to maintain an aesthetic consistency, as the administrative vestry had done at St Nicholas.

In the Holy Name chapel there are two windows, dedicated to St Joseph and St John the Baptist. Although they are of the same proportions as the disciple sequence, they appear to be of an older provenance, (note the gothic lettering) and from a different artist. At the edge of the first photograph of the church, a window of similar size is shown in the west wall at the end of the south aisle. This wall, behind the present organ, is now filled in, but one can still clearly see the outline of the window arches. This is where I believe the St John and St Joseph windows were originally housed. They would have been moved to the Holy Name Chapel at the time of the expansion in 1881-3.

In the Tower Chapel, formerly the Chapel of the Transfiguration, which served as an oratory, where the Blessed Sacrament was first reserved in the church, there are two cruder stained glass windows, which are latched, and can be opened. They must date from 1886, the time of the original formation of the chapel. They depict the Transfiguration and the Presentation of the Gifts by the Magi. The Sisters of Bethany and of the Holy Name used this oratory as their prayer chapel, and it continued to function as such well into the Sixties. In time, the church hopes to restore this sacred space to its original function.

In the vestibule created at the time of the building of the church tower, there are windows depicting two of the Evangelists, Mark and Luke. Matthew and John are included in the sequence of apostles, so it seems likely that these are of later provenance, intending to complete the set of four, probably dating from 1892 when F.T. Cawthorn (Edmund Scott's associate) added the tower.

The Sanctuary

The sanctuary was re-ordered under Father Tiley, and it reflects his taste for the baroque. He gifted the reredos which was designed by Martin Travers around 1930, (see the discussion of its shortcomings above) and also the Jacobean-style screens. The High Altar is a much grander affair than that which graced the original church. As well as the golden tabernacle for the Reservation of the Sacrament, and a superfluity of golden candlesticks (some of which were among the artefacts 'kidnapped' in 1903), it now accommodates four reliquary busts of the apostles, Paul, Thomas, Phillip and Barnabas, and two monstrances which contain 'sacred' remains. These tiny ossified relics are displayed in glass capsules in the chests of the saints. The busts have unbroken paper seals on the back. I have not been able to ascertain who purchased them and brought them to the Annunciation, but they feel generic and mass-produced.

To either side of the Burne-Jones window, there are two Annunciation ceramic panels, copies after Della Robbia, in the characteristic blue and white of the artist.[1] There are also two terracotta plaques of the Annunciation and the Visitation.[2] These were given in memory of Sister Elizabeth SSB who led the Mission House in Lincoln Street. She died in 1908. A small plaque to Sister Elizabeth's memory is affixed to the wall joining the sanctuary and the Chapel of the Holy Name. Above it is a memorial, from 1937, to Father Davis in whose memory the current Stations of the Cross, distributed along the walls of the church, were given. The originals, 'praised' by Bishop Durnford at the celebration Mass for the consecration of the church in 1884, and visible in an early photo of the mission, have now disappeared.

The rood figure of Christ crucified on the vine is also noteworthy. It appears that two images are compounded here, that of the Crucifixion and of Christ as the vine. The biblical passage the work refers to is John 15 1-5 beginning: 'I am the true vine', but it is unusual to see Christ crucified in this manner. However, Christ's crucifixion upon the vine was a popular image on sixteenth and seventeenth century broadsheets, so it is not without precedent. Ironically it also assimilates the image of Bacchus from pre-Christian belief, surely not an allusion that Father Tiley intended.

There is another mystery here. The figure of Christ on the Vine picks up a theme first elaborated at the Annunciation in the memorial page, printed in the Parish Magazine in January 1896, to mark the death of Father Fison. Here, Christ is depicted crucified on a wine-press. It is a remarkable print, and it begs several questions. Did this image have a particular currency in the Oxford Movement, and was Father Tiley availing himself of this tradition? Or was he (or the artist he commissioned) familiar with the Fison memorial? When we compare the images, the similarity cannot be a coincidence, even though, on the rood, the image has become more simply the vine, rather than the wine-press.

The Holy Name Chapel

There are two statues of note in the Holy Name Chapel. The wooden statue of St Francis of Assisi is the work of Mother Mirabelle of the Community of Saint Mary the Virgin, Wantage (c. 1924). It was restored in the 1990s by Joy Doble, a popular and insightful member of the congregation. The Statue of Our Lady of Walsingham reflects the Annunciation's close associations with the Norfolk shrine, to which there is an annual pilgrimage.

Both these statues came to the Annunciation from the Convent in Rottingdean, whence the Community of the Blessed Virgin Mary (a sisterhood of nuns which Arthur Wagner had founded in Brighton in 1855) had removed in 1977, and which had finally disbanded in 1983. The provenance of the statue of Joseph is unknown.

The icon of the Resurrection below the windows was commissioned from a visiting Rumanian icon painter in the early 2000s. It is executed in the generic Byzantine tradition, but it contains a striking image of Mary Magdalene greeting the risen Christ.

The Nave and Tower

The most revered statue in the church is the figure of the Blessed Virgin Mary. It was commissioned by the church, during Father Hinde's time, in memory of his predecessor Father Fison, to whom it is inscribed on the base. It was erected and dedicated on the Feast of the Assumption 1896 (the day chosen by Arthur Wagner for many significant events at the church since its opening on that day in 1864). We have followed the statue of the Virgin's eventful history in Chapter 7 of this book.

Beside the Stations of the Cross, there are a number of significant artworks hanging in the nave. I have mentioned Gherado della Notte's *The Adoration of the Shepherds* elsewhere in this history. It is dated in the copyist's hand to 1912, although the original date looks as if it has been rubbed out and overwritten. The copy licence, signed by the superintendent of the gallery, still adheres to the back of the canvas. It has recently been cleaned and restored by Joe Michel, revealing for the first time, the sacrificial lamb hung around the central shepherd's shoulders. The Annunciation has the Mafia to thank for increasing the value of this copy. The original painting no longer exists. In 1993 there was a bomb attack on the Uffizi Gallery during a Mafia feud, and Della Notte's painting was virtually obliterated.

On the South Wall hangs an aquatint of one of Rubens' four altarpieces for Antwerp Cathedral. The central panel of the triptych shows the Deposition from the Cross. The left side panel depicts the Presentation of Christ in the Temple, the right side panel shows the Visitation. The chronology of the original has been reversed. This may be due to the fact that the frame is inscribed with the three events in the wrong order, leaving the framer with no choice but to reverse the chronology of the panels. An oddity. Joe Michel has suggested to me this might be the work of the engraver Valentine Green, whose three mezzotint plates were printed in colours around 1800. The frame is contemporary with that date – the black and gold embellishment (verre églomisé) was a short-lived vogue precisely at that time.

The Roll of Honour next to the War Altar was commissioned by Father William Carey, immediately after the First World War. It is illustrated on vellum. The memorial lists the fallen from the whole community of Hanover. Only a small number of the forty servicemen named here were regular members of the congregation.

In the Tower Chapel, formerly known as the Chapel of The Transfiguration, there is a hand-coloured print of Murillo's *Madonna and Child*, in a similar style of frame to the Della Notte. The original, painted around 1650 is in the Pitti Palace in Florence. It is another example of Counter Reformation art in the church. We do not know the donor of any of these works, but successive vicars of the Annunciation were regular visitors to Italy, and these may be souvenirs of those visits.

Inside the Tower, the original bells hang, silent now for over sixty years, awaiting renovation. The Angelus bell rings out on Sunday just before Holy Communion, and immediately after the Mass when the Angelus is recited or sung. The bell was restored and rehung in 1947 in memory of Evelyn May Wilkinson, a long-standing member of the congregation.

Some noteworthy memorials

It might seem odd that the memorial marble plaques to George Chapman and Reginald Fison, its revered first vicars, are on either side of the entrance from the vestibule to the present church. In Chapman's case, the positioning is appropriate because it marks the spot where he was afflicted with the haemorrhage that killed him, as he was drawing aside the curtain on his way into the oratory (see Edwin Green's description in Chapter 4). It was Green, described by One of his People as 'his loved and trusted friend, his faithful fellow worker of more than ten years' standing', who placed George Chapman's memorial here. One senses his hand too in the positioning of Father Fison's memorial nearby five years later. These are, in any case, the first inscriptions one reads on entering the church.

Below Chapman's memorial, above the water stoup, is a tablet in memory of James Medhurst (Jim), the churchwarden, who had volunteered for service in 1915 (see Chapter 8). A great servant to the church in peacetime and war, he died in 1949.

Note also the memorial tablet to Father James Gatley who was assistant priest from 1889-1896, and captain of the Annunciation cricket team. He died in Tasmania in 1914. Appropriately, over the present-day crèche, is the memorial to Charlotte St John, 'a most faithful and devoted servant to the church', who took great care of the children of the parish, and was their Sunday School teacher for three decades. It is to her that we owe the first atmospheric memories of the mission, and it with her, who seems always to have been at my shoulder while I have been writing, that I end, for the present, this history of the Church of the Annunciation.

NOTES TO THE TEXT

Introduction

1) The Roman Catholic Relief Act gave Roman Catholics a place in English society long denied them. But to many it seemed a first step towards the disestablishment of the Church of England. This fear was heightened in the 1840s when the Peel administration proposed that the grant to the Maynooth Seminary in Ireland should be increased and made permanent. Many Protestants saw the use of public money in this way as the government giving Rome a foothold in the establishment. The so-called 'Papal Aggression' of 1850, when Pope Pius IX was allowed to set up setting up a Roman Catholic diocesan system in England and Wales, met with fierce Protestant resistance, and led to the creation of many militant Protestant Associations. This gives us some of the context for the vehement opposition to the Annunciation in its early days.

2) The term 'The Oxford Movement' was as much defined by its subsequent followers and opponents, as by those who began it. I have used the term here to cover the period of the Catholic Revival in the Church of England from John Keble's seminal speech of 1833 on 'National Apostasy', delivered in Oxford, and generally regarded as the beginning of the movement, into the late nineteenth century when the movement merges and becomes indistinguishable from Anglo-Catholic practice and theology.

3) The Cambridge Movement was led by John Mason Neale (1818-1866). While still an undergraduate, he co-founded the Cambridge Camden Society (later renamed the Ecclesiological Society) in 1839. It was nominally set up to promote 'the study of Gothic Architecture and of Ecclesiastical Antiques', but it was later largely responsible for adapting the theological ideas of the Oxford Movement into a programme of aesthetic renewal and liturgical reform. It also encouraged the foundation of Anglican orders, such as the Community of the Blessed Virgin Mary which Arthur Wagner founded in Brighton in 1855. Neale penned many great Anglican hymns and hymn translations including *Good King Wenceslas* and *All Glory Laud and Honour*.

4) The Annunciation was not the first mission that Wagner founded. In 1862 he had already opened the Church of St Mary and St Mary Magdalene in Bread Street, Brighton. It was demolished around 1950.

5) Arthur Wagner, however, should not be seen as an exception in this regard. Only one of the fourteen writers of the original Tracts seceded to Rome. The majority of the Oxford Movement remained deeply loyal to the Church of England.

1. The Mustard Seed

1) 'Laine' is an old Brighton tenantry term used to denote a large tract of agricultural land.

2) These houses were built in Whichelo Place, Islingword Road, Islingword Place and Park Street. The tenants were charged affordable rents.

3) At this time, the churches were given public money to provide education for the poor. Many people still remained hostile to the idea of mass education, imagining it would expose the working class to seditious ideas. Neither did the church want to lose its influence over local youth. Even after the introduction of the Elementary Education Act in 1870 which made provision for elementary education for 5 to 13 year olds,

several hundred children were still catered for in the Annunciation Schools. Thereafter, Arthur Wagner, and the priests of the Annunciation kept a close eye on the staff and curriculum, as if it were still part of their estate.

2. Pussybites

1) This insistence on auricular confession proved contentious for Wagner during the Constance Kent affair in 1865, when Wagner was publicly vilified for refusing to answer in court questions pertaining to a confession given to him by Constance Kent. Kent had murdered her four-year-old step-brother five years earlier, but there was insufficient evidence to commit her for trial. She had come to reside at St Mary's Home in Queen's Square, Brighton, as a paying guest of the Community of the Blessed Virgin Mary. Deeply effected by the religious atmosphere of St Mary's Home, she confessed the murder to Wagner and, eventually, with her consent, this confession was made public. Wagner was suspected of having pressurised Constance Kent, and he was subsequently hissed in court at Kent's trial when he refused to answer two questions about the circumstances surrounding her confession. So strong was the feeling in the town against him, a police guard had to be mounted on St Mary's Home and on Wagner's own house.

2) As the Catholic Revival gathered momentum in the final quarter of the nineteenth century, increasing pressure was brought to bear on ritualists. In 1874, The Public Worship Regulation Act was introduced by the Archbishop of Canterbury, Archibald Campbell Tait, to limit the growing ritualism in Anglo-Catholicism. Five priests were imprisoned nationally. One of these was Father Richard Enraght, an ex-curate of Father Wagner's at St Paul's. He was prosecuted in the Court of Arches in 1880 under the act for the ritual use of 'wafer bread' as a sacrament. Enraght was a Tractarian. While under Wagner at St Paul's he had published the acclaimed pamphlet *Who are True Churchmen and who are Conspirators?*, asserting the historical rights of the Catholic clergy. In 1872, while Vicar of St Andrew's Portslade, he had published a contentious pamphlet entitled *The Real Presence and Holy Scripture*. which had antagonised the Church Association. Enraght refused to recognise the legitimacy of the court and did not attend his trial. He was found guilty, given the maximum sentence under the act, and was imprisoned in Warwick Prison. The Court of Appeal released him on a technicality after 49 days, but his actual appeal in the House of Lords failed, and the authorities still attempted to have him returned to jail. The case led to a Royal Commission in 1881 which studied the case, and led to the abandonment of the prosecution of ritualistic priests when it reported two years later. The Public Worship Regulation Act was subsequently regarded as a failure in curbing ritualism, because it had created Anglo-Catholic martyrs, thus actually strengthening the revival. This mechanism was clearly enduring. In 2006, Brighton and Hove Council honoured Enraght as a 'Priest, fighter for religious freedom'.

3) A friend of Matthew Arnold, Charles Anderson had literary ambitions, and produced several books, including a semi-autobiographical novel. He deplored the schism between ritualists and evangelicals, and gradually grew closer to the 'Broad Church'. An interesting and undogmatic writer, Anderson provides a sanguine view of the rift in *Catholicism*, an essay he contributed to his Soho anthology *Words and Works in a London Parish (1873)*.

3. Father Chapman

1) This is not to say that George Chapman was in the business of encouraging conversion to Rome, as the following account from an early mission he conducted shows:

   During this mission in Manchester, a person attending it said to Mr Chapman, 'I wish I had been brought up a Roman Catholic, it would have been happier for me!' He rose from his seat, and with righteous indignation, said with some sternness, 'How can you say that?' and then more calmly, and in his usual gentle, but forcible way, went on to say he could not imagine how any earnest Churchman could leave the English Church for the Roman communion. papal usurpation, and the latest interpretation of papal infallibility, and he might add, the untheological devotions to our Lady encouraged by modern Romanism alone alone ought to prevent secession.

2) R.S. (we do not have her full name) wrote *George Chapman – a Narrative of a Devoted Life,* the only biography of Father Chapman. It was published by Swan Sonnenschein and Co in London in 1893, less than two years after his death. The book was edited by the Reverend Alfred Gurney (1845 – 1898), vicar of St Barnabas, Pimlico. During the time he was a curate in Brighton, Gurney had developed a close friendship with Chapman. A minor poet, he was also a friend to the Beardsley family.

3) Chapman also established a Perseverance Guild, with separate wards for men (St Joseph's Ward), women (St Monica's Ward) and for boys and girls. These were meetings for moral instruction following Mass. In addition, he promoted membership of the new Anglican devotional society The Guild of All Souls (founded in 1873), dedicated to prayer for the departed, and to teaching the Catholic doctrine of the Communion of Saints.

4. Expansion

1) In R.S.'s biography of Chapman the date is clearly given as 1880. She also speaks of the 'three years' of Chapman's curacy, i.e. before he became vicar. It makes sense that the church became a parish before the expansion; and it also explains why Father Chapman chose to remain at the Annunciation as vicar rather than curate when offered the incumbency of St James the Less in 1882, on the death of the Reverend Bramah. Most histories, including the church's own centenary book in 1964 have given the date of parish status as 1888. This error may stem from the Jubilee Book of 1914, in which Charlotte St John (or her typesetter) gives the wrong date.

2) The Sisters of Bethany were to remain in the Annunciation until 1952.

3) Had plans for a separate school for girls been realised, the intention was to assume the normal east/west axis of the church by removing the floor, thus creating a high ceiling, and placing the altar at the Washington St end. Instead, the present axis was retained.

4) The observance of the Stations of the Cross was being performed at the Annunciation by 1871, one of the earliest examples of this practice in the Church of England.

5) This slim volume of recollections was introduced by the Reverend John Baghot-De La Bere, the vicar of St Mary's, Buxted. 'One of his People' also included extracts from some of Father Chapman's sermons. It was published by Oxford: Mowbray & Co., Church Printers in 1892.

6) George Chapman's tomb in the cemetery was vandalised in April 1983, but it appears to have been a mindless rather than sectarian attack.

5. The Real Presence

1) Reservation had been permitted in *The Book of Common Prayer* in 1549, but then prohibited in the revised version in 1552. In 1662, the rubric of the prayer book of 1562 was altered to insist that after the communion the remains of the sacraments were to be 'reverently consumed'. Thereafter sacramental reservation was discontinued amongst Anglicans until the 19th century.

2) In Tract 90 of the *Tracts for our Times*, published in 1841, John Henry Newman argued for a more relaxed interpretation of Article XXVIII of the Thirty-Nine Articles.

3) The interpretation of the Real Presence shifted over time among the Oxford Movement scholars. Initially, the Tractarians did not insist on a literal understanding of transubstantiation, but in the mid- and late-nineteenth centuries, the practice of Reservation and Exposition in churches like the Annunciation seems to have objectified the Real Presence and made the interpretation increasingly literal.

4) In 1854 J.M. Neale founded one of the first Anglican order of nuns at Sackville College (almshouses for the poor) at East Grinstead where he was the warden, and this was later housed in the Convent of St Margaret, East Grinstead. He reserved the Sacrament in the Convent Chapel. In his book *Fashions in Church Furnishings*, Peter Anson writes:
   > Dr Neale bought a small tabernacle in London and placed it on the altar, and started continuous Reservation of the consecrated elements. By 1858 he had acquired a monstrance, and familiarised his growing community with the extra liturgical Roman rites of Exposition and Benediction.

5) R.S. is, of course, referring to the use of Reserved Sacrament in extremis here, and says nothing about Exposition or Benediction.

6) One of Aubrey Beardsley's biographers, Malcolm Easton, writing in 1972, goes so far as to suggest that Arthur Wagner was using George Chapman as an agent provocateur:
   > Making a spearhead of The Annunciation, Wagner had no doubt selected a fanatical Ritualist whom, in case of trouble, he would have delighted in backing against his Bishop.
   These assumptions reveal how little insight Mr Easton had gained into the characters of both George Chapman and Arthur Wagner.

7) Arguably, the oldest Anglo-Catholic devotional society, the Confraternity of the Blessed Sacrament, (motto: Adoremus in aeternum sanctissimum sacramentum), was founded in 1862 to affirm belief in the Real Presence, and to promote adoration of the Reserved Sacrament amongst Anglicans.

8) A prominent memorial to Cecil Wray was placed under the Oxford Movement window at the Annunciation during the renovation 1881-3 (see page 105).

9) In the last hundred years, Reservation has become increasingly widespread in the Anglo-Catholic tradition and even in some centrist churches of the Church of England. Permission is still required from a bishop for the permanent Reservation of the consecrated elements of the Eucharist. Where the Blessed Sacrament is reserved, it must be kept in a place approved by the bishop. The Sacrament is now reserved in an aumbry in the Lady Chapel in Chichester Cathedral. Church history is not wanting for irony.

10) The continuation of the quotation is interesting, with regard to the makeshift arrangements during the expansion:

The accessories of the Service became matters of little importance – although of course we did our utmost to dignify the Blessed Sacrament to the extent of our power – and whether the Celebration was in the poor old Annunciation or the new and glorious Annunciation, or even in the upper room of the Boys School in Southover Street (as it was for some weeks during the re-building), it was the Presence that was the only thing of real importance.

11) R.S. tells us the first Eucharist was celebrated in this chapel on August 6th 1886.

12) In the latter part of his tenure, Father Hinde held Benediction every Thursday. After his departure, it continued under Father Carey, but was known euphemistically as 'Intercessions'. It continued thereafter, under different names, and was preceded once a month by a meeting of the Confraternity of the Blessed Sacrament. It was not until Father Tiley's time that it was known as Adoration. Benediction is still celebrated on high holidays at the Annunciation today, such as Corpus Christi.

13) John Hawes, in his account 'Ritual and Riot', published in 1995, suggests that there is some evidence the Blessed Sacrament was reserved at the Annunciation 'as early as 1884', the year of the church's dedication. But he also puts the date of the creation of the parish erroneously in 1884.

14) The next earliest Reservation is given by Yates as St Margaret's Liverpool in 1878.

6. Gathering Clouds

1) On the death of Bishop Durnford in 1895, Father Fison wrote:

At the death of Father Chapman, the Bishop expressed his wish that things should be carried on on the same lines, and though there were not wanting those who tried, conscientiously enough no doubt, to make mischief between the Bishop and us, they were never rewarded with any success.

These remarks show us the beleaguered state of the Annunciation even during Father Chapman's time, but it also makes clear the Annunciation did not see the Bishop as the opposition. Father Fison, at least saw him as the defender of his Marian style of faith.

Some years ago at a meeting in Brighton, language was used of the Blessed Virgin Mary which could not but pain and scandalise every one who had any love for our Lord. We remember how the Bishop came forward and sternly rebuked those misguided men. He is not sorry for that now! Love and honour for Mary will help us in and after the hour of our death.

In the same article, we can hear the contempt in which Father Fison held state interference in the church:

The appointment of Bishops by the Crown is a shameful abuse and a grave scandal.

This was very much the view of his employer, Arthur Wagner, and of the Oxford Movement in general.

2) Hinde kept the full Roman *Kalendar* of daily Eucharists for Easter Week in 1896, his first year as vicar. Puzzlingly, both John Hawes in *Ritual and Riot* and Father Bullivant in his Centenary Booklet of 1964 attribute the introduction to the Annunciation of full Roman rites at Eastertide to Hinde. But the Parish Magazine for April 1895 clearly advertises the Triduum (for the first time) in the last year of Father Fison's incumbency. Bullivant writes:

Having taught the people that as Catholics they were entitled to the privileges of the Catholic Faith, he (Hinde) proceeded to make them available, and in Holy Week 1897 (sic) the ceremonies of Maundy Thursday, Good Friday and Holy Saturday were celebrated for the first time at the Annunciation. Fr Fison had intended to introduce them during his last year but the honour fell to Fr Hinde.

Similarly, and perhaps basing his assertion on Bullivant's, Hawes writes:

His incumbency was to be troubled, and the first signs of difficulty appeared in 1898. As Fr Hinde had introduced the full Roman Holy Week ceremonies the year before, again one of the very earliest instances of this, these problems were not altogether unexpected, as Protestant resistance to ritualistic services was being stirred up on a national level by one John Kensit.

I have been unable to find the sources for these assertions. Unless, both writers are referring to additional ritual during Easter Week, (still today the Annunciation congregation processes to venerate the cross during the Good Friday Mass, and on Easter Saturday a fire ritual precedes the vigil) rather than additional services, it appears they are both mistaken, and the 'honour' had already fallen to Father Fison.

3) Edwin Green was a minister at the Annunciation for more than fifteen years, under both Fathers Chapman and Fison. He was presented with a purse containing seventy guineas by the parishioners when he left the Annunciation in 1896.

4) The transition of the Annunciation Schools to the state happened gradually. They were not finally ceded until 1903, when the management was fully devolved to a committee comprising members of the local authority and a new Foundation set up to support the schools. The connection between the church and the schools was finally severed by Father Hinde. He was the last priest to chair the management committee for the church, and in 1904 he declined to be part of the Foundation.

By now, the Brighton Education Committee was exercising more and more scrutiny over the schools, and it was only a matter of time before they were fully absorbed into what was then known as 'the provided schools'. In 1905, at the request of the Education Committee, the Annunciation schools were closed and, with the eventual consent of the managing committee, the children were transferred to new 'provided schools'. The days of education being directly controlled by the church were over. Thereafter, the Boys School building in Southover Street became an infant school with no direct affiliation to the church. Yet the building itself was not finally sold off to the local authority until the early 1930s. The proceeds from this sale were eventually used to fund the building of the Mission House in Lincoln Street, on a parcel of land adjoining the schools that Arthur Wagner had given to the church in trust in 1894.

7. Henry Hinde's Journey to Rome

1) It is remarkable how, over time, the Annunciation became a temple that memorialised its own priests.

2) The crisis reveals the flourishing congregations of the Anglo-Catholic churches in Brighton in 1910. Pouring oil on the flames, *The Tablet* observed on 10th September:

No one acquainted with the Annunciation and St. Bartholomew's can doubt that

Mr. Hinde and Mr. Cocks have suffered keenly during the past few weeks. To build up, in one case what is probably the largest congregation in the Diocese, and in the other case a congregation as large as the church will hold, and then suddenly break with all—it would not be human to undergo such an ordeal without an acute pang of regret. But even harder, perhaps, is the lot of the congregations, thus bereft of the spiritual guidance to which for so many years they have been accustomed. It is not too much to say that a feeling of desolation and deep perplexity prevails at St. Bartholomew's and the Annunciation. The congregations have done everything they possibly could do to retain their vicars, and now that they are at the end of their resources the most profound anxiety is felt as to what may happen in the future.

3) A rather telling juxtaposition appears in the notes section of *The Tablet* for the 10th June 1911. It is rather sloppily edited, but surely not coincidental:

Next Tuesday the international Pontifical Church of St. Joachim will be solemnly consecrated. It forms a splendid memorial of the Episcopal Jubilee of Leo XIII. and of the many chapels decorated by the various nations that of the Blessed Sacrament, the gift of England, is one of the handsomest.—Next Sunday in the Pauline chapel in the Vatican his Eminence Cardinal Merry del Val will raise to the subdiaconate: (1) Henry Fitzrichard Paul Hinde, M.A., Cantab., lately Vicar of Our Lady of the Annunciation, Brighton; (2) his curate, Henry Rhodes John Mary Prince, B.A., Oxon.; (3) Arthur Reginald Carew Bernard Cox, (sic) M.A., Oxon, lately Vicar of St. Bartholomew's, Brighton; (4) his curate,(sic) Ernest Reginald Francis Shebbeare, B.A., Oxon.; (5) Oliver Partridge Alphege Henly, B.A., Oxon., and (6) John Henry Steele, M.A., T.C.D., lately Chaplain to the Earl of Erne.

Shebbeare was curate at the Annunciation under Hinde, not under Cocks at St Bartholomew's.

4) There are currently two statues of Joseph at the Annunciation. One is pictured in Davey's photograph. The other is not in the photograph, and may postdate the kidnap. It has never, to anyone's knowledge, left the church. R.S., Chapman's biographer, mentions the following: 'a beautiful statue of the Good Shepherd was placed in memory of the late mission by the organ'. This statue is in the postcard photograph of the kidnapped statuary, but now it seems to have disappeared from the church. It is possible that the Good Shepherd, and not St Joseph, went with Father Hinde, and the story has been confused because of his later attachment to St Joseph's Catholic Church.

5) It is interesting to note that this anticipated by a century The Personal Ordinariate of Our Lady of Walsingham, the mission established by Pope Benedict in 2012, which allowed Anglicans departing the Church of England to enter into full union with the Catholic Church while retaining much of their heritage and traditions.

8. The Great War

1) It was left to the assistant priest at the Annunciation, the Reverend Mainwaring, to keep the half-deserted ship afloat after the triple secession. This he did admirably; and he continued to support the succeeding vicars of the Annunciation for many years, an

unsung figure of continuity at a time of great sorrow for the church.

2) Sir Arthur Conan Doyle wrote of the battle in which Walter Greed fell:

Never in the history of the world had a more formidable force been concentrated upon a fixed and limited objective. The greatest possible expectations were founded upon the battle, which had already been named the "Kaiserschlacht," while the day chosen had been called Michael's day, or the day of Germany's revenge.

10. Decline

1) Although Father Tiley did occasionally return to the Annunciation to preach for Father Power.

2) The Mission House still belongs to the church today. The Sisters of Bethany occupied it from its opening in 1939 until 1952. After living in cramped local houses in the parish since their arrival in 1882, the nuns were pleased to have purpose-built accommodation. One feature was irksome, however – the retrieval of balls kicked over the wall from the schoolyard in Southover Street. After the departure of the Sisters of Bethany, the Mission House was occupied by the Sisters of the Holy Name who served the church from 1954-1973. Thereafter, from 1978, it was occupied for a number of years by members of The Order of the Glorious Ascension, the monastic order set up by Bishop Peter Ball, the former Bishop of Lewes. Today it is rented from the church by a housing association. Because of the original stipulations of the trust under which that lease is held, the premises must be used for educational purposes.

3) The objections were:

- The Annunciation wished to remain with the Wagner Trustees.
- The church refused to replace Choral Eucharist with Sung Mattins.
- The P.C.C. explained that they had funded the building of the Mission House for the Sisters of Bethany in 1939 without applying for any financial help from the Diocese.
- St Martin's were served by a different order of nuns.
- The church viewed with grave concern the proposed demolition of St Luke's, Queen's Park (*still thriving today!*), because it would make the area unworkable with the proposed number of priests and sisters.
- If an amalgamation was unavoidable, the church wished to be grouped with St Bartholomew's.
- A substantial amount of work needed to be done on the fabric of the church, and the churchwardens felt they could not proceed with this in the current uncertainty.

11. Rocky

1) In 2010, during the interregnum, a further attempt was made by the Diocese (subsequent to the one made in the early 1950s) to amalgamate the Annunciation with St Bartholomew's. The respective P.C.C.s met, but neither showed enthusiasm for the merger. The proposal was eventually shelved by the Annunciation P.C.C., a majority of whom voted for 'further deliberation'.

12. Father Bullivant

1) In the early Fifties, Father Bullivant also greatly encouraged the in-house drama group, the Annunciation Players, who had begun meeting regularly at the church after the war, putting on their own productions in the Coleman Street Hall. The company was run by a husband and wife team – Ivor and Joan Pelling. They wrote and produced the shows themselves, usually murder mysteries, and even toured them to Brighton General Hospital. Father Bullivant wrote a review of their production of *The Contest*:

   > *In these days of Television and Radio and Cinema it is a pleasant relief to get back to the informality and friendly atmosphere of the family entertainment which was so much part of home life thirty or so years ago, and we all look forward to another pleasant evening in the near future when I hope we shall have the hall full.*

   But Father Bullivant was also doing some casting of his own. He confirmed the thespian Pellings in April 1954, and thereafter Ivor Pelling was a sidesman in Father Bullivant's regular Sunday show. The tradition of producing drama comes and goes at the Annunciation. Father Chapman was not a fan of the drama. When asked if he thought it wrong to go to the theatre he replied: 'I don't say wrong, but much better not, There is quite enough sin in the world. You and I commit quite sins enough without 'inventing' any more'. Drama is nevertheless currently thriving again at the Annunciation. The current congregation boasts a significant number of theatre professionals – notably Roger and Jenny Alborough and Janet Hewlett-Davies. A new play *The Gospel According to Lilian,* featuring the above, will be produced to mark the 150th anniversary of the church.

2) This seems odd, given Bishop Bell's previous disinclination towards the Marian style of worship at the Annunciation. It may merely have been a formulaic request, however. We may remember that Bishop Durnford had requested the same continuity of Father Fison, after the death of Father Chapman.

3) Father Bullivant's notes read:

   > *I said I hoped that she did not think we were Roman Catholic. I hoped we had a balanced teaching. Stress was laid on evangelism of Mission service. People fully taught that B.V.M and Mass were nothing in themselves.*

4) I only have the draft of this letter, and I am only assuming it was sent.

5) The Community of the Holy Name was founded in 1865 by Father George William Herbert (1830-1894), parish priest of St Peter's Church, Vauxhall, London, with the intention of ministering to the poor.

6) Ironically, the saint one prays to when things are lost.

7) According to his granddaughter, Rosemary Faulkner Mitchener (a current member of the congregation) David Bishop was christened in the church in 1887, during Father Chapman's incumbency.

8) Martin Morgan is the long-serving vicar of Rottingdean.

9) Father Bullivant wasn't afraid to spend money on the fabric of the building when it was necessary, however. His meticulous attention to every detail of the church building is evident from the church records. But he didn't stint on liturgical luxury either, boasting an opulent collection of vestments, and claiming that one set were made from the coronation robes of Tsar Nicholas I.

13. Father David

1) And establishing the new tradition of the congregation referring to priests by their Christian names – i.e. Father Steven, Father Michael etc.

2) Another initiative that Father David and Jane Launchbury set up together at the church was called 'A Space to Be'. Jane Launchbury writes: *This was a multi-faith group, also open to those of no faith, who wanted to share experiences, live music, silence and the joys and tragedies of life and have a beautiful sacred space in which to just be.* This initiative was later progressed by Peter Pannett and Judy Greenfield, leading lights of the Annunciation's spiritual life in the early 2000s. They both subsequently became deacons.

3) Jane Launchbury remembers the early Hanover Days, before the culture of public liability and health and safety:

   My recollection was that Hanover Day was actually completely instigated by the church, not the community, and for years it was a devil of a job to get the community to take part in the organising or fundraising at all. I was heavily involved from the start, but I probably saw myself as part of the church by then, albeit not as a formal communicant member. The first ever Hanover Day was a phenomenal undertaking and covered many more streets than recent ones. The statues came out of church and Our Lady was processed all over the place, zig-zagging along streets up the hill, not just around out of the front door of the church and back in through the vicarage garden. Though I have a vague idea that this procession was technically illegal both in church and civil terms. We even had donkey rides in the Mission House garden!

14. The New Millennium

1) It is no coincidence that the pre-Raphaelite movement was roughly contemporary with the Anglo-Catholic church-building of the mid-nineteenth century. They had similar intentions – a return to pre-Reformation models (hence the commissioning of the Burne-Jones/William Morris window at the Annunciation). The revival was similarly dominated by a return to the Gothic and to the Romanesque in church and school architecture. The Chapel of Lancing College, founded in 1868, is a prime local example of the former.

2) This was, I believe, Father John B. Eskrigge, who left the Church of England and the Annunciation for Rome around 1881. He was ordained as a Catholic Priest in September 1883. He is listed in the second edition of *Converts to Rome - a list of about 4000 Protestants*, compiled by W. Gordon Gorman in 1885, and published with a prefacing letter from William Gladstone. An intriguing letter, signed by Eskrigge appeared in *The Tablet* in October 1900, entitled 'A Warning':

   SIR,—I should be obliged if you would be kind enough to allow me to warn your readers against a person who is using my name to obtain money under false pretences. She is of middle age, has very plausible manners, and talks piously. She generally produces a letter card written by me some time since to her husband as a proof of her being known to me as a reliable person.

3) Herbert Hamilton Maughan, born in 1884, was the author of several books on Anglo-Catholicism. *Wagner of Brighton*, *Some Brighton Churches*, and *The Anglican Circus*. In the

1920s, commissioned by Father Tiley, he wrote 'a fairly large history' of the Annunciation. Remembering this 30 years later, he claims he was paid £20 for the commission. Father Tiley never had it published 'because the cost would have been higher than he bargained for', Hamilton Maughan writes to Father Bullivant, and continues:

Although he paid me liberally for the work, which involved a good deal of research and hard work, I was very sorry that it was never published, as it was a very complete history. I have no doubt that he still has the typescript somewhere.

Given Hamilton Maughan's subsequent conversion, it would make fascinating reading, if it still exists.

4) George Bell resolutely opposed the carpet-bombing of German cities, and in 1944 spoke out against it in a famous speech in the House of Lords, resulting in much vilification, both during and after the war. Bishop Bell urged the government to make a distinction between the Nazis and the German people. In Noël Coward's *Don't let's be beastly to the Germans*, we find the lyrics '*Don't let's be beastly to the Germans/Now our victory is ultimately won/Let us treat them very kindly/As we would a valued friend/We might send them out some Bishops/As a form of lease and lend.'* This is generally supposed to refer to Bishop Bell.

5) A core of worshippers in the Annunciation still retain a belief in the Apostolic Succession, and in the idea that the power of creating the miracle of transubstantiation has been handed down through an unbroken line of male priests since St Peter. In deference to them, the church has kept resolutions 'a' and 'b', debarring women from either presiding at Holy Communion, or becoming the incumbent or priest-in-charge. A third resolution 'c', which would have put the church under a Provincial Episcopal Visitor, commonly known as, a 'flying bishop' to safeguard them against the oversight of a female bishop, was never adopted. Nevertheless, the continuing adoption of 'a' and 'b' has left the Annunciation as part of a church minority which is out of step with the rest of society in terms of gender equality. So far a compromise has been maintained between the differing views in the church. But these resolutions are soon to wither away, to be replaced in the Church of England by a system under which a parish has to request, by letter, special governance by a flying bishop. In the present author's view, it is unlikely the Catholic traditionalists would be in the majority in the present congregation at the Annunciation in supporting such a request. Despite these differences, there is an acknowledgment of the investment of faith that has been practiced by the traditionalists in the church. It may therefore be many more years before this issue is resolved. The question remains, however, whether it will then be too late to engage the next generation in the ritualistic religion the Annunciation offers, because this will be inseparably associated with gender inequality.

The Music of the Annunciation

1) Though it is part of the Apocrypha in other traditions, Catholics accept Ecclesiasticus as a deuterocanonical scriptural text.

2) Father Chapman had a phenomenal memory for people's birthdays. The day before their anniversary, each member of the choir would be invited to join him for communion. They would then be presented with their gift – 'this was given in the vestry, and a few kind, helpful words and a formal blessing accompanied it' (R.S.).

3) Chapman enjoyed these outings, even taking part in the races while he was still in good health.

4) Nevertheless, Father Hinde must have had some fondness for music beyond the church. In 1909, for example, he organised an exotic Grand Bazaar and Café Chantant at the Royal Pavilion in aid of charity. On the bill for this grand event, attended by 'the quality', were such artists as: Miss Hannah Fuggle, Miss May Eckhoff, Countess Marie Zolawolaska, Madame Carmen and Mr Harold E. Taylor. There was also a display of costume and 'fancy dancing', and Father Hinde, ever fond of reproductive technology, showed lantern slides of Switzerland.

5) Fred Sayers and his wife Peggy, much loved members of the congregation, have now been commemorated in a new set of hymn books, financed by the legacy they left the church.

The Art of the Annunciation

1) *The Panels at the High Altar are reproductions by Messrs Cantagalli, of Florence, of a celebrated work by Andrea Della Robbia (15th century), at the Altar of the Annunciation in the Franciscan Conventual Church of La Verna, where St Francis received the Stigmata; it is situated about thirty miles east of Florence. They represent to Mystery of the Incarnation: in one is a half-length figure of the Blessed Virgin engaged in meditation; in the other the Angel Gabriel kneels in adoring wonder as he delivers the message of God. In the base of the Panel is a rose, signifying her title of 'Rosa Mystica'; and below the Angel is a fleur-de-lis, symbol of purity.* I have this information from the Parish Magazine for July 1909. The style is unmistakably that of Father Hinde, who must have introduced them.

2) *The Panels at the Altar of the Holy Name are plaster reliefs, designed and made by a modern Italian artist, Signor Manzoni, and coloured under the direction of the Art and Book Company, of London. One represents the Annunciation, and the other the Visitation; in the latter St Elizabeth kneels before our Lady to receive the salutation at the door of the house, her husband, Zacharias, standing by.* The source is once again the Parish Magazine for July 1909. Both descriptions confirm the drift of Henry Hinde's thoughts southwards at this time.

Index